For Jessie Cruickshank discipleship isn't ar[...]
In this insightful book, Jessie fuses a biblic[...]
discipleship with the taxonomy of Joseph [...]
Journey and shows us how spiritual matur[...]
of learning and unlearning, being broken and remade. Or to use her
words, it is "climbing the mountain and coming back down again."
Here's the guidebook to get you started on that heroic journey.

MICHAEL FROST, founding director of Tinsley Institute at Morling College in
Sydney, Australia

So much of what we are seeing in today's church behavior in and
outside of the building can be linked to discipleship (or the lack
thereof). This simple, practical, and inspiring book is needed in this
time to help ordinary people like you and me join in on an amazing
opportunity and privilege that we are actually made for . . . that of
making disciples of Jesus. Jessie provides helpful insights, stories,
and even brain science to point the way for us to lean into a God-
given invitation to be agents of transformation for lives around us.

REV. DR. ELIZABETH RIOS, founder of The Passion Center and
Passion2Plant Network

Discipleship is a word that often haphazardly gets thrown
around in the church. Definitions are numerous; achievement
is rare. Though this book title uses the word "ordinary," it is an
extraordinary call to the true north of the church . . . making
disciples who also make disciples. Jessie does a tremendous job
of serving as our guide through the journey of not only being a
disciple but teaching others to be guides as well.

ROWLAND SMITH, national director of Forge America Mission Training
Network, author of *Life Out Loud: Joining Jesus Outside the Walls of the
Church,* curator/editor of *Red Skies: 10 Essential Conversations Exploring
Our Future as the Church*

"Not biologically possible." The words leapt off the page as
Cruickshank described the most common discipleship method
I have seen attempted all my life. *Ordinary Discipleship* clearly
guides us to change the way the brain learns the life of the Spirit.

JIM WILDER, PhD, neurotheologian, author of *Renovated: God, Dallas Willard,
and the Church That Transforms*

My friend Jessie Cruickshank lives and believes what she writes. As a church leader, it has been a long time since I've read such a practical resource for those in disciplemaking. The church needs this work. In fact, while this book is itself accessible and "ordinary"—the words here are paradigm-shifting and world-changing. You'll leave these pages equipped, encouraged, and ready to start your own adventure of ordinary discipleship. A must-read for all who want to lead others in following Jesus.

AUBREY SAMPSON, MA in evangelism and leadership, church planter and teaching pastor, author of *Known: How Believing Who God Says You Are Changes Everything*

Recently, there's been a lot of buzz around brain science and discipleship. What does this mean? How does it intersect? What can we do differently? In this book, you are going to find the answers to these questions, but it's not going to be in the way that you might initially think. Jessie offers a practical and accessible framework to easily help you leverage the insights from brain science into discipleship and disciplemaking. It's amazing. Don't miss this important work.

DANIEL IM, lead pastor at Beulah Alliance Church, podcaster, author of several books, most recently *You Are What You Do: And Six Other Lies about Work, Life, and Love*

Jessie Cruickshank is the dangerous sort. She robs the intelligentsia of vital concepts they attempt to obfuscate and makes them visible and usable to everyday people. *Ordinary Discipleship* is a bit of sleight of hand. Jessie takes a hidden and seldom-used concept, priesthood of the believer, and makes it operational for the average Joe and Sally. Dare I say that it is a breath of fresh air to read not only because she uses her outdoor experience as metaphor from cover to cover but also because the ever-abiding references operate like superglue, attaching the concept to concrete, doable actions. I am roped up and ready to use this tool!

ROY MORAN, visionary of Shoal Creek Community Church, author of *Spent Matches*, chairman of New Generations

In this refreshing look into the hows and whys of discipleship, my friend Jessie Cruickshank brings some unique insights from brain science together with a spirituality of adventure to provoke everyday believers to hit the road of discipleship again. A very readable and engaging book.

ALAN HIRSCH, award-winning author on missional theology, spirituality, and leadership; founder of Movement Leaders Collective and Forge Missional Training Network

Ordinary Discipleship is the product of Jessie's heart as a genuine disciplemaker, her mind as a brilliant strategist, and her hands as a literal wilderness guide! Jessie helps you help others move from thinking of discipleship as just a boring pathway to seeing it as a lifelong, practical adventure filled with valleys and summits, as well as relationships and revelation.

DANIEL YANG, director of Church Multiplication Institute at the Wheaton College Billy Graham Center

In *Ordinary Discipleship*, Jessie Cruickshank pulls from her years of experience as a wilderness guide to drive home this much-needed truth: that all of us are meant to be disciplemakers, and that we all have opportunities to do so no matter our place in life. *Ordinary Discipleship* is a much-needed guide for anyone ready to embark on this foundational adventure of discipleship!

DAVE FERGUSON, visionary leader for NewThing, author of *BLESS: 5 Everyday Ways to Love your Neighbor and Change the World*

"We determine how much of the Kingdom we experience." Jessie weaves the journey of transformational discipleship, explaining the critical waypoints between the relational Trinity calling all believers to make disciples and a disciple experiencing the Kingdom in community here on earth as it is in heaven. Jessie lays out strong practices and tools with anchoring principles applicable in a multitude of settings and contexts. This book is a wonderful field guide to disciplemaking.

KRISTIE TURNER MONTEIRO, mission director of Disciplemakers for Life at The Navigators

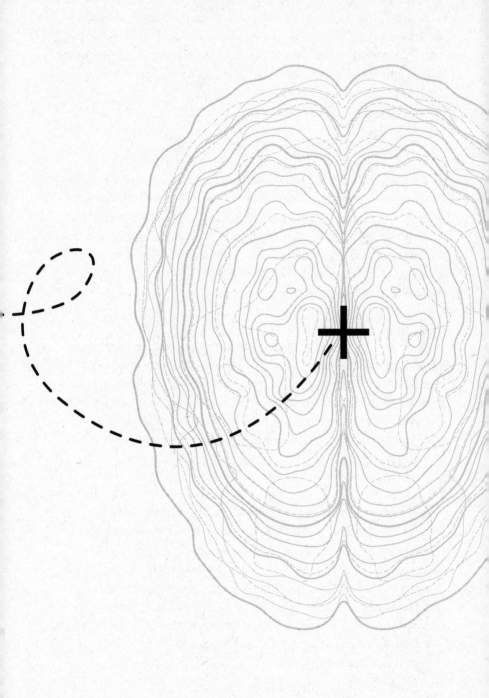

Jessie Cruickshank

ORDINARY DISCIPLESHIP

HOW GOD WIRES US FOR THE ADVENTURE OF TRANSFORMATION

A NavPress resource published in alliance
with Tyndale House Publishers

NavPress is the publishing ministry of The Navigators, an international Christian organization and leader in personal spiritual development. NavPress is committed to helping people grow spiritually and enjoy lives of meaning and hope through personal and group resources that are biblically rooted, culturally relevant, and highly practical.

For more information, visit NavPress.com.

Ordinary Discipleship: How God Wires Us for the Adventure of Transformation

Copyright © 2023 by Jessie Cruickshank. All rights reserved.

A NavPress resource published in alliance with Tyndale House Publishers.

NavPress and the NavPress logo are registered trademarks of NavPress, The Navigators, Colorado Springs, CO. *Tyndale* is a registered trademark of Tyndale House Publishers. Absence of ® in connection with marks of NavPress or other parties does not indicate an absence of registration of those marks.

The Team:
David Zimmerman, Publisher; Caitlyn Carlson, Acquisitions Editor; Barbara J. Scott, Copy Editor; Olivia Eldredge, Operations Manager; Sarah Susan Richardson, Designer

Cover illustration of brain copyright © anastad/Depositphotos. All rights reserved.

Illustration of sunset icon by Alice Design/The Noun Project.

Illustration of backpack icon by iconbysonny/The Noun Project.

Illustration of flashlight icon by Vitaly Gorbachev on icons8.com.

Illustration of boot print icon by Pastel Glyph on icons8.com.

Author photo by Julia Schmaltz, copyright © 2021. All rights reserved.

The Author is represented by the literary agency of WordServe Literary, www.wordserveliterary.com

Scripture quotations marked ESV are from the ESV® Bible (The Holy Bible, English Standard Version®), copyright © 2001 by Crossway, a publishing ministry of Good News Publishers. Used by permission. All rights reserved. Scripture quotations marked MSG are taken from *The Message*, copyright © 1993, 2002, 2018 by Eugene H. Peterson. Used by permission of NavPress. All rights reserved. Represented by Tyndale House Publishers. Scripture quotations marked NIV are taken from the Holy Bible, *New International Version,*® *NIV.*® Copyright © 1973, 1978, 1984, 2011 by Biblica, Inc.® Used by permission. All rights reserved worldwide. Scripture quotations marked NLT are taken from the *Holy Bible*, New Living Translation, copyright © 1996, 2004, 2015 by Tyndale House Foundation. Used by permission of Tyndale House Publishers, Carol Stream, Illinois 60188. All rights reserved.

Some of the anecdotal illustrations in this book are true to life and are included with the permission of the persons involved. All other illustrations are composites of real situations, and any resemblance to people living or dead is purely coincidental.

For information about special discounts for bulk purchases, please contact Tyndale House Publishers at csresponse@tyndale.com, or call 1-855-277-9400.

ISBN 978-1-64158-732-7

Printed in the United States of America

29 28 27 26 25 24 23
7   6   5   4   3   2   1

To those who discipled me and taught me what that meant:
Mom, Dad, Drew, Mary, Joe, Allison, and Steve.
And to SROM (Solid Rock Outdoor Ministries), Andrew
and Josh, who are my brothers in Christ and served with me
while we were just "hoods in the woods." God has been very
generous with his instruction, revelation,
and abounding grace.

LIVES CHANGED

EXPERIENCES REVELATION

LEARNS NEW THINGS

FEELS THE STRUGGLE

TEAMS WITH OTHERS

ANSWERS THE CALL

ORDINARY PERSON

DISCERNS THE SEASON

Contents

Foreword

Why read a book about making disciples? If you're anything like me, you're probably thinking that we've exhausted every formula, strategy, or program available—and to be totally honest, the success rate has been less than impressive. We all know we are supposed to do the last thing Jesus commanded his disciples to do, but most of us dread the whole idea, thinking it is something we are not qualified or gifted enough to do. As a result, we are often filled with shame, guilt, or condemnation because of our perceived inadequacy and sadly end up spending most of our lives as Jesus followers doing lots of secondary things—all the while missing the joy of doing the actual thing we are all called to do. But I truly believe that only our misunderstanding of what it is to make disciples has resulted in our unwillingness or inability to do so.

Jesus said, "Therefore, go and make disciples of all the nations, baptizing them in the name of the Father and the Son and the Holy Spirit. Teach these new disciples to obey all the commands I have given you" (Matthew 28:19-20, NLT). With these words, he invites us into the greatest adventure on this side of eternity. He is not calling us to adopt and implement a behavior-modification program, nor is he calling us to disseminate information to people as if they are computers who need more data for their memory bank. Rather, he invites us to embark on a breathtaking journey, to know him more intimately, and thus to become more like him.

Jesus has not given us a command that he has not equipped and empowered us to fulfill, nor has he asked us to do something that would not be an integral part of the abundant life he came to give us. Disciplemaking is not an obligation, but the greatest privilege of our lives—and it is for everyone, not just the "special ones." If we understood how vital our own part is in fulfilling the Great Commission, and then did our part, we would actually fulfill the Great Commission. It's not rocket science. It's disciplemaking.

It was over dinner that Jessie first shared with me the concepts she has unpacked in *Ordinary Discipleship*. I remember thinking then, *Everyone needs to hear this message*. This is not a how-to manual; it is a guidebook that makes you want to embark on the adventure that is disciplemaking. Jessie not only demystifies the process of making disciples, she offers us a road map—unique for each person—to do the very thing we are called to do.

Jessie's passion and conviction poured out on these pages are contagious. I believe that more is caught than taught in life, and you will catch the heart of disciplemaking in this book. Jessie lives, eats, and breathes this message, and she is the most pragmatic mystic I have ever met. As we journey through this blend of biblical truth, brain science, outdoor adventures, and the power of story, we are left with an insatiable desire to be, and make, disciples of Jesus.

This is the book on making disciples that I have been waiting for—and I know you have too.

CHRISTINE CAINE
*Founder of the A21 Campaign
and Propel Women*

Acknowledgments

Special thanks to all my friends and fellow sojourners whose stories and wisdom are shared in these pages. You are some of my greatest teachers; you inspire me.

Thank you to all those who helped me move this project from inception to completion: Anna Robinson, Rowland Smith, Julia Schmaltz, Bob Cruickshank, Caitlyn Carlson, and the team at NavPress.

A final shout-out to my local Panera Bread for letting me occupy a booth for countless hours with a Pellegrino and a muffin.

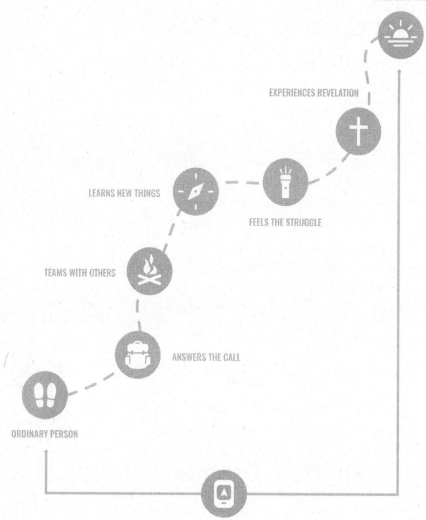

LIVES CHANGED

EXPERIENCES REVELATION

LEARNS NEW THINGS

FEELS THE STRUGGLE

TEAMS WITH OTHERS

ANSWERS THE CALL

ORDINARY PERSON

DISCERNS THE SEASON

EXPERIENCE THE JOURNEY

Becoming a Hero Maker

May the God of peace . . . equip you with everything good for doing his will.

HEBREWS 13:20-21, NIV

DREW ARNOLD WAS THE FIRST PERSON to recognize the call of God on my life. I was going to be a high school science teacher, but the spring after I graduated from college, a phone call from Drew changed all my plans.

Throughout high school and college, I had professionally guided wilderness expeditions for different organizations. One of those was Drew's organization—Solid Rock Outdoor Ministries. SROM was similar to Youth with a Mission, only stateside in the deep trails of Wyoming; instead of going on a mission trip, students learned about God in the wilderness.

Drew asked me if I would work full time for SROM. I prayed about it for one week (which is crazy short for me—I dated my husband for five years), before saying yes to $350 a month to build this wilderness school for disciplemaking.

Drew had been an amazing rock climber, wilderness mountaineer, and skier, but now he had multiple sclerosis and was
confined to a wheelchair. That didn't stop his fervent pursuit
of the call of God, though. He had stepped down from his full-
time pastoral role to lean into being a mentor and disciplemaker, choosing to spend his days pouring into me and his
son, Andrew, and eventually another leader named Josh as
we worked to build SROM.

In this season of leadership, I was out of my league,
in over my head, and desperate for Jesus. Knowing how
dangerous our work could be, I decided I needed to figure out how to teach something once with a high degree
of effectiveness so that someone could remember it with a
high degree of accuracy. Lives depended on it. That's when
I began studying and reading about how the brain learns
and changes.

But what began as a risk-management exercise, I realized,
had disciplemaking implications as well. Many times, I would
have only ten minutes to an hour with a student. How could
that one conversation be effective enough to possibly change
eternity?

I started applying the science of transformation to the art
of disciplemaking. I took everything I'd been learning about
the brain and placed it over questions like:

- *How do you have a disciplemaking conversation?*
- *How do you hear what God is doing?*
- *How do you partner with God so that in five minutes
  something catalytic can happen and someone's life
  can change?*

At SROM, we began paying attention to people's transformation stories, discovering we could predict when change was likely to take place and what we were doing to either help or hinder the process. We adjusted our program to best facilitate transformation.

Not everyone changed, but many did. They could choose to be willing participants in the transformation or not.

Fascinated by these revelations, I went on a sabbatical from SROM to obtain my graduate degree in Mind, Brain, and Experiential Education—and what I discovered was the science behind what God had already shown me:

God hardwired our brains for transformation, which means anyone can help anyone else on the journey to change.

Agents of Transformation

Everything that has happened in your life—every aha moment, insight, or healed wound—has equipped you for the task of making disciples. You don't need to have lived another life or be a different person. You just need to look at your life through God's eyes. He has equipped you. You are hardwired for transformation, and you are created to be an agent of transformation.

Discipleship, like being a wilderness guide, is about helping people choose to go somewhere they have never gone before or do something they have never done before. *It is about helping someone be brave enough to choose to change.* It is showing them a new way of living in the world and exploring what they have never seen. It is sharing wisdom—not general wisdom, but the hard-fought wisdom *you* have learned in the life of faith—and teaching skills so they can do it on their own. Both can feel like a blind walk into the unknown, but you'll find that it's the journey, not the destination, that matters most.

In the Bible, the Greek word for disciple is *mathetes.* Literally translated, it means *learner.* But the problem in our Western mindset is that we associate learning with the mind, reason, and information. Take it from the educational neuroscientist, this is a dangerous misunderstanding. Education is important, but it has *limits*—things it can do and things it can't.

True learning is deep and holistic. It affects all parts of us—body, soul, and spirit. We are not transformed by facts and information, but by what we believe in our bones. If our life does not demonstrate it, we have not learned it. So, being a learner in the biblical sense is about apprenticing our lives to Jesus and choosing to live changed by what we learn.

In guiding others, success is not defined by whether we conquer the mountain, but by whether we conquer our inner fears and self-imposed limitations. Discipleship is not simply about whether we make it to heaven when we die, but how our encounter with the risen Jesus changes us today. Jesus transforms our fears into faith and our weaknesses into his strength throughout our lives. This grace is a free gift, not of ourselves (Ephesians 2:8). Through the great love of Jesus, we are changed. We live in relationship with Jesus, remaining attentive to him and obedient to what he asks us to do. Our relationship with Jesus alters our lives. As we follow his guidance, our motives, actions, and behaviors change. The great joy of discipleship is helping others be changed by Jesus too. As we share life together in a messy world, we extend his example, simply sharing with others how Jesus has transformed our own lives. We help people to walk in love and obedience as Christ transforms them too.

The innate transformation of the journey of faith is why anyone can be a disciplemaker. If you have given your life to Jesus, you have your own journey of transformation to share!

So, now that we've talked a bit about disciples and disciplemakers, let's adopt some better definitions:

- A **disciple** is someone who chooses to be changed by their relationship with Jesus.

- A **disciplemaker** is a disciple who lives changed by Jesus and journeys with others for the intentional Spirit-led purpose of helping them be changed by their relationship with Jesus too.

God loves us exactly where we are. But he also paid an exceedingly high price for us to live in greater freedom and intimacy with him. He is always trying to move us into a greater fullness of life, which is why he has provided guides and companions to help us. Disciplemaking happens when a person partners with God in this process and becomes a voice of love and truth in our lives.

I have been on hundreds of wilderness adventures. Whether we were walking, camping, climbing, or resting, our true selves were being revealed. We were exposed and reshaped by what we faced and by each other. I remember John, a skinny, sassy kid who talked a big game. He thought sarcasm and emotional distance made him a leader. But as we stood on the edge of the Grand Canyon, all that bluster faded. On our twenty-mile journey down to the river, John learned that he could open up to the community. In serving others, he had the tangible experience of being a leader and a hero. When we returned seven days later, John's parents did not recognize their son.

Often, by the end of a wilderness trip, students were no longer students but overcomers and heroes who had faced their challenges. And I was no longer a guide but a hero maker, someone who had helped others discover who they were and what they could do.

That's what it is to be a disciplemaker. We take a person from where they are to where they have never been. We help guide them from who they are to who God created them to be.

The Hero's Journey

You may know the story. Frodo Baggins, called out of ordinary life in the Shire, is tasked with carrying the Ring of great power to the volcano where it was made. He initially rejects the task, believing he is ill-equipped for such a significant and dangerous undertaking. Only when he realizes that he is the only one with a heart strong enough to resist the evil of the Ring does he agree to take on the assignment. Many others accompany him, including his best friend, Samwise, who never leaves his side. The journey is filled with friends, enemies, mentors, and challenges for Frodo to overcome both physically and in his own heart.

Whether or not we're acquainted with *The Lord of the Rings*, the outline it follows is familiar. We might notice the same pattern with Luke Skywalker in *Star Wars,* or Neo from

The Matrix, or countless other characters from our favorite movies and books. It resonates somewhere deep inside us. We identify with the struggle, the fear, the need for friendship, and the need for help. We understand how the desire for the known and the comfortable can battle against the call to the unknown and the turbulent journey ahead.

Real heroes suffer and face danger with courage. They don't start out as heroes; they become heroes. Their journey changes them and takes them to places they would never have chosen to go on their own.

I suspect you've heard this story. You have lived this story. You have read this story in a hundred books and seen it in a hundred movies.

In the 1940s, Joseph Campbell researched the great mythic[1] stories in human history and found a consistent pattern across cultures and civilizations. Despite being separated by continents and thousands of years, each culture's epic story followed the same pattern.

Campbell named this pattern *The Hero's Journey,* and it is taught in story-writing classes all over the world:

- A hero is called out of his or her ordinary world and presented with an insurmountable challenge.
- The hero initially refuses the call, usually due to feelings of inadequacy.
- With the help of a mentor, allies, and friends, the hero embraces the task at hand.

---

[1] To be clear, *mythic* does not necessarily mean "fantasy" or "false." *Mythic* means "epic." These stories often communicate the morals and values of the culture.

- Along the way they face considerable opposition and trials.
- Finally, the hero obtains the reward and returns to their ordinary world, transformed by their experience.

Something about the Hero's Journey inspires us, calls to us, and awakens a deep longing inside of us.

Think about your own journey for a moment. Where did a moment of real transformation and change take place in your relationship with Jesus? It likely came at a point of despair or adversity. You probably did not wake up that morning with the thought, *I really want to become a better Christian today.* But life presented you with a circumstance that catapulted you to change.

Sometimes we get to choose our journey and sometimes we don't. In fact, sometimes the journey is forced upon us, like when we find out we have cancer or someone close to us dies, or when our job takes us to a different state and we have to move. We can't always determine the circumstances we find ourselves in.

Our choice then becomes whether we will participate in the transformation. Will we answer the call and say yes to what God is doing?

PERSONAL REFLECTION

What is a circumstance or opportunity that you said yes to that changed you?

I believe God wrote this pattern, this Hero's Journey, on our hearts and on all human hearts, so that we would know what he wants for us. It helps us recognize the path, even when we don't know the way. But it is more than that. It is also our blueprint, our outline so that we can come alongside someone and help them become a disciple. It is the map for the journey of a disciplemaker.

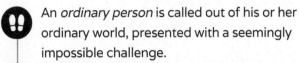 An *ordinary person* is called out of his or her ordinary world, presented with a seemingly impossible challenge.

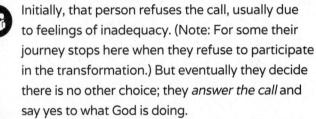 Initially, that person refuses the call, usually due to feelings of inadequacy. (Note: For some their journey stops here when they refuse to participate in the transformation.) But eventually they decide there is no other choice; they *answer the call* and say yes to what God is doing.

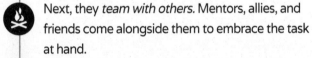 Next, they *team with others.* Mentors, allies, and friends come alongside them to embrace the task at hand.

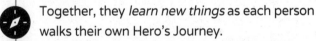 Together, they *learn new things* as each person walks their own Hero's Journey.

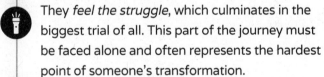 They *feel the struggle*, which culminates in the biggest trial of all. This part of the journey must be faced alone and often represents the hardest point of someone's transformation.

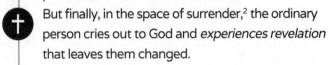 But finally, in the space of surrender,[2] the ordinary person cries out to God and *experiences revelation* that leaves them changed.

---

[2] In the words of Isaiah the prophet, "'Woe to me!' I cried. 'I am ruined! For I am a man of unclean lips, and I live among a people of unclean lips, and my eyes have seen the King, the LORD Almighty'" (Isaiah 6:5, NIV).

Ultimately, something in the ordinary person's life is redeemed and restored. This is what makes them a hero. As they return to their ordinary world, the ordinary person has become a hero and *lives a changed life*—transformed by their experience.

Once we know what to look for, we see the pattern of the Hero's Journey everywhere in the life of faith.

The Hero's Journey is woven throughout Scripture. This is Abraham's story and Moses' and David's and Ruth's and Mary's. It is Paul's story and Peter's story.

Disciplemaker Pro Tip: Jesus himself modeled the perfect Hero's Journey. He knows the path and invites us to follow him as our guide. When you get lost, look to him to help find your footing.

We see the Hero's Journey in the Israelites leaving Egypt through the Red Sea, going into the desert, and eventually entering the Promised Land. We see it in their journey into exile. Any time you leave, are recreated, and return, you have completed the Hero's Journey.

This is the journey we all take as disciples. We are all on this map somewhere. And every season of learning from God follows this pattern, so we experience it over and over. As you look at the map and understand the journey, you will recognize it in your own life and be able to identify where you are as a disciple. Learning to orient yourself on the map won't just help you, it will help everyone who wants to be a disciple or a disciplemaker.

An Ordinary Person Answers the Call

At the beginning of every story is not a hero, but an ordinary person sitting in the middle of ordinary life. Jesus always starts with regular people. In Luke 5:1-11, we see this stage mirrored in the life of Peter, who was working as a simple fisherman when Jesus showed up on the shore. Suddenly Peter's mundane world was disrupted, awakening something deep inside. But Peter had responsibilities, a family.

Multiple times Jesus gave the invitation to "follow me." There was a rich young man who asked Jesus what he must do to follow him. Jesus said he needed to leave everything (Mark 10:17-27). Jesus told another young man to leave his parents (Luke 9:59-62). Both young men chose to end their journeys with Jesus right here. They chose to remain in life as they knew it.

When everyday life is disrupted, we are faced with a choice and a decision. And almost all of us initially "reject the call." The cost is too great, we have too many responsibilities, we are afraid. Approximately 50 percent of people end their journey right here before it ever begins.[3]

Peter, too, initially rejected the call. He "fell at Jesus' knees and said, 'Go away from me, Lord; I am a sinful man!'. . . Then Jesus said to Simon, 'Don't be afraid; from now on you will fish for people'" (Luke 5:8, 10, NIV). What a crazy invitation! Did Peter even know what it meant? Probably not. And yet we know that although Peter's initial response was no, he eventually answered the call with a yes.[4]

_____

[3] James W. Fowler, *Stages of Faith: The Psychology of Human Development and the Quest for Meaning* (New York: HarperCollins, 1981), 318, Table B.3.

[4] Download a free example of Peter's Hero's Journey at ordinarydiscipleship.com.

We each have the world we know—the "normal" that we wake up to each day. It is in this very place, the ordinary place, that Jesus calls us to step out and follow him as a disciple. Jesus did not limit his invitation to the religious leaders. He invited fishermen, tax collectors, women, and the marginalized as well. The invitation to follow Jesus is given to the ordinary person who will answer the call with yes.

PERSONAL REFLECTION

Think about your own call to follow Jesus. What was your "ordinary world"? What was your response? Have you left the safety of your pre-Jesus world to follow him?

Teams with Others to Learn New Things

Once the ordinary person accepts the call, she quickly learns that she is not alone. God always brings others to accompany us on our journey—mentors, guides, allies, and friends. Soon, alongside these companions, the ordinary person learns the skills, tools, or character traits required for the challenges ahead. This knowledge is gained through the day-to-day happenings of life: learning to hear God's voice, prayer, studying Scripture, and growing in the fruits of the Spirit. For Peter and the other disciples, this happened as they learned from Jesus in community. Jesus also gave his disciples opportunities to practice what they were learning. He sent them out two by two (Mark 6:7-12), and he used life's opportunities as teachable moments.

Likewise, Jesus uses community to reveal our strengths

and weaknesses. We learn what gifts we have and what we bring to the table to give others. We also discover areas where others are more mature or competent and what we can learn from them. Jesus works with us to develop our character toward increasing Christlikeness and living in the Kingdom of God through community.

PERSONAL REFLECTION

Think about your Jesus journey. Who has been with you on this? Who has mentored you? Who has been your friend? What impact have they had on you? Would you take a Hero's Journey if you had a band of friends and a mentor to walk with you?

Feels the Struggle and Experiences Revelation

It's the big scene in all our favorite movies; the main character faces the moment where they either fail or transition from ordinary person to hero. For Frodo, that moment was when he chose to relinquish the Ring to the fire of Mordor. The moment usually happens in the middle of significant struggle, as the ordinary person wrestles with who they are supposed to be and what they are supposed to do. Music swells, tensions rise. And then—breakthrough. Out of the fire, a revelation—clarity about who that person is created to be.

Peter experienced the struggle when he denied Christ and the rooster crowed. In denying Jesus, Peter had done what he said he would never do. His sense of self was shaken. His grief was profound. So he returned to being an ordinary fisherman.

Until—revelation. The resurrected Jesus stood before him, holding love, restoration, and breakfast in his hands.

Testing can come in many forms. We may be tempted to compromise our character to take shortcuts in our jobs. Or we might have to surrender our specific vision for how a family event should go so that everyone can work together to build a better plan. The real trial requires us to face our fears, overcome a temptation, or renounce a false belief about God and embrace truth.

Jesus promises us that testing is part of the process of growth. Paul writes that fire exposes the quality of our faith (1 Corinthians 3:11-15). But testing is meant to reveal beauty. As a disciple we follow Jesus into hard places. We follow him into the valley of the shadow of death. And the greatest way we overcome is when we discover joy in the midst of challenge. The trials in our life help refine and purify us, making us stronger, more connected to each other, and more effective for the Kingdom. We sit with our friends as Jesus prepares a table before our enemies, and in those moments we realize how strong we are together. And no matter what we face, Jesus will never leave us, and Holy Spirit[5] will always be there to guide us.

PERSONAL REFLECTION

In your Hero's Journey, what is a fear, temptation, or false belief you have overcome? How did that happen? Who was there and helped with that overcoming?

---

[5] Have you ever wondered why, when we talk about God and Jesus, we call them by name, as people, but then we talk about the third person of the Trinity like a thing? You'll notice that I talk about Holy Spirit as the third part of the Godhead, without the word "the." I'm not insisting on this for you, but as we talk about Holy Spirit in this book, know that I've left the word out and call Holy Spirit by name. Try it yourself!

Lives Changed by Jesus

In the final phase, the ordinary person has completed the Hero's Journey and become a hero. The hero reflects upon how she has changed, the relationships she has built, and the revelation she has gained. She often says goodbye to her mentor and allies, returning to the same ordinary world where she started. But the world is different—not because *it* has changed but because *she* has changed.

Most of us would never think of joy, peace, hope, faith, and self-control as our sources of power against worldly tensions, injustice, and division. However, Scripture tells us that is exactly what we are given as tools (2 Corinthians 10:4). These are the prizes God's Word promises we will find on our journey of discipleship. And they are amazing gifts, like a spring of water hidden in the desert, or the ruckus of laughter that rises up around a campfire. These gifts are strong and trustworthy. When we discover and develop the gifts on our journey, we'll find that they are not easily stolen from us. And the deep relationship that we build with God and with our companions is something that will exist for all eternity. This is how we are transformed—and how we transform the world.

PERSONAL REFLECTION

How were you a different person on the other side of a trial? In your own journey of overcoming, what treasures or prizes have you gained? What truths about God or fruits of the Spirit have been deposited in you as a real, tangible treasure?

Your Guidebook

In my decade as a wilderness instructor trainer, I read hundreds of guidebooks—everything from laminated maps on the South American Andes and the Utah desert rivers, to typed Word documents detailing the climbing area of my first ascents. The descriptions in guidebooks can be a little mysterious, and you have to take them with a grain (or handful) of salt. Descriptions of climbs or river rapids, for example, are often puzzling and even poetic: "*Whether you climb the face or the hand crack (at this point), the number of grunts remains fixed.*" You might read the words a few times and wonder, "What does that mean?"

Guidebooks intend to create intrigue because their purpose is only to get you to the river, the rock face, or the base of the mountain. They do not give a step-by-step account of the route. For one, that would ruin the adventure of it. Second, routes change. A river is never the same from one day to the next. Rocks move, glaciers travel, and the environment is evolving and migrating. Giving a step-by-step description of the path would lure the reader into a false sense of confidence, control, and complacency. And in the outdoors, complacency causes death.

Consider this book your guide to disciplemaking. It won't give you step-by-step instructions, mainly because no two discipleship relationships are the same. Instead, this journey we're going on together is meant to get you to the base of the route. You'll learn foundational principles that help you see the larger picture of relational disciplemaking so you can find your way. But that will take us a little time—and a little trust—as we walk the path.

This book is written for you, the disciplemaker, the guide, even if you don't yet see yourself as that. It is meant to help and equip you for that role, though it won't be your only text on the topic. Like all guidebooks, this book is limited by the lens of personal experience. So I have included some actual standard guidebook disclaimers, adapted for context:

- Disciplemaking is a hazardous activity. Proceed at your own risk.
- You are responsible for your own actions.
- A specific person may, in fact, be harder to disciple than this book indicates.
- Do not be lulled into a false sense of security because you have read this book.
- Mileage was measured on my life's odometer. Personal experience of mileage may vary.
- The reader releases the author from liability of any harm that may result from this activity.

Every guide has their first trip. If you have never discipled anyone, begin to pray for God to prepare your heart (and theirs) for the journey ahead. You are called to make disciples just as you are—with your face, your story, and your gifts. With your strengths, your weaknesses, your revelations, and your misunderstandings, you are called right now to make disciples. I pray that in this book you will find the simple encouragement and practical equipping to convince you of that Kingdom-forming truth.

And if you're feeling daunted by the journey ahead, I want you to consider—what if . . . ?

What if every person who believed in Jesus as Lord embraced the Great Commission to make disciples? What if they saw the people they encountered daily, at work and in their neighborhoods, as potential Jesus followers on a journey? What if they started praying for some of those people regularly and listened to what Holy Spirit was saying about them?

What if every Jesus follower spoke words of hope that refreshed the soul and connected with people at a heart level? What if each Jesus follower intentionally mentored another person in the things of Jesus—sharing their life and wisdom with someone else?

Discipleship would once again be the life-giving, community-impacting, world-changing adventure Jesus always intended it to be.

The explosion of spiritual gurus, self-help communities, and life coaches in contemporary culture shows us that we're hungry to be mentored and poured into. When each one of us embraces our part of the disciplemaking tapestry, we can help meet this need to be shaped by love. Then the world will see a rich, accessible, and wondrous Jesus and the beautiful simplicity of abundant life with God.

Discussion Questions

Before you can guide someone else on their journey, you need to map out your own. Think about a testimony or revelation you had with God and answer the following questions.[6]

---

[6] You can download a free template of the Hero's Journey questions at ordinarydiscipleship.com.

1. (Ordinary Person) Where were you at in life? What was your starting point?

2. (Answers the Call) What did the call God placed on you look like? How did you respond? What did you have to overcome to start your journey?

3. (Teams with Others) Who did God bring to join you on your journey?

4. (Learns New Things) What sort of things did God teach you?

5. (Feels the Struggle) What obstacles or challenges did you have to face?

6. (Experiences Revelation) What truths, insights, and revelations did God give you?

7. (Lives Changed) How are you different because of your journey?

Inventory

In every chapter, we're going to pause to reflect and capture insights about that stage of the journey. Your inventory will equip you for the steps ahead.

At the beginning of the chapter, we looked at this Scripture passage:

> May the God of peace . . . equip you with everything good for doing his will.
> HEBREWS 13:20-21, NIV

How does the Scripture sound to you now? What new meaning does it carry for you?

What revelations or insights are you taking away from this chapter? Capture them here:

Revelation/Insight #1

Revelation/Insight #2

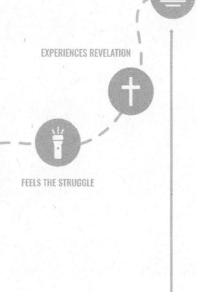

LIVES CHANGED

EXPERIENCES REVELATION

LEARNS NEW THINGS

FEELS THE STRUGGLE

TEAMS WITH OTHERS

ANSWERS THE CALL

ORDINARY PERSON

DISCERNS THE SEASON

2

AN ORDINARY PERSON

The Journey of Disciplemaking

The members of the council were amazed when they saw the boldness of Peter and John, for they could see that they were ordinary men with no special training in the Scriptures. They also recognized them as men who had been with Jesus.

ACTS 4:13, NLT

IT WAS A WEDNESDAY NIGHT at my home church, the first time a cohort was working through the Ordinary Discipleship online class together. My church is ethnically diverse, full of salt-of-the-earth people, only some of whom are college educated. The group of twenty-four was truly a Kingdom cohort—a mix of high-school students, elders, pastoral staff, young adults with developmental delays, a homeless evangelist, and everything in between.

What overwhelmed me, though, was not their presence. Listening as they shared their answers to the initial framing questions—*What is a disciple? What does it look like to be a disciplemaker?*—I found myself stunned by their wisdom.

They answered these questions plainly; discipleship meant following Jesus, helping someone else follow Jesus, praying with people, and being in relationship with people.

I have asked these same questions in many rooms, with many pastors, and few grasped these simple yet profound truths. The answers from those that many would consider "experts" are often complex and leave them tripping over their own convictions.

Here, on this day, I was in awe. These ordinary, often overlooked people innately understood the Kingdom. It brought me to tears—and the class had barely even started. In this room, I got a glimpse of a vital truth: that ordinary, everyday people have and always will be God's plan A for the Great Commission.

God-Sized Ache

How many times during a normal day do you find yourself scrolling through your social media feed to see what is happening in the lives of other people? We observe the food they eat, the projects they are working on, videos of their kids, or the vacations they take. Inevitably, feelings of comparison creep in. We wonder, *Am I living as I should, or is there something more I should be doing?*

We all have an internal ache and desire to be part of something bigger than ourselves. For many of us, we attempt to alleviate this ache with vicarious adventure, whether that be through movies, books, Netflix, or social media. The TV schedule is full of "reality TV" and adventure shows. But how often do we settle for virtual reality instead of actual reality?

Unfortunately, living vicariously through other people's adventures will only dull the ache for our own; it will never satisfy us.

We each have a God-ache that reminds us we desire to have an impact on our world. This ache creates a posture toward a cosmic yes and helps us be brave enough to know that while we are yet ordinary, we are also capable of the extraordinary.

PERSONAL REFLECTION

Why do you think we ache to do something great or be someone influential? What do you think God may want to do with that desire?

Anyone Can Make Disciples

We know Jesus says we are supposed to make disciples (Matthew 28:18-20). But how many of us really feel confident to effectively disciple another person? The culture in the church would demonstrate that not many of us think we can. I don't believe it is because we do not care enough or we are not smart enough. Rather, I think it is because we have complicated what should be simple. Modern-day Christianity has turned discipleship into a complex system of processes, and of course that makes most Christians feel unqualified. They feel like they must be spiritual superstars, know all the answers, do it alone, or have their life together.

Disciplemaking, at its essence, is simply about helping a person discover who God says they are and helping them live into it. In trying to do that in safe and sanitized classrooms or through individual study, we have lost the wild path of authentic Kingdom discipleship. Most of the time, we're not even sure we have the right map. And many of our clues for what discipleship includes—like the need to understand the Bible—can actually lead us further away from discipleship as Jesus intended it to be.

Recently I was sitting across the table from a mature and capable pastor bemoaning the state of discipleship in the American church. Let's call him Jim. As we talked, he stopped and looked at me curiously. "Sermons, books, and tapes . . ." he said, reflectively, "they are not discipleship. They are *teaching*."

"Exactly!" I replied. "Because discipleship is a relational thing, not a content thing. It can never be discipleship if there is no relationship."

He told me later that this was a light-bulb moment for him. He had been in ministry for forty years, building and maintaining a decent-sized congregation. Jim believed in leadership development and had moved the people in his congregation from passive consumerism to becoming more active and engaged with the ministry of the church. And yet, Jim realized that day, he'd been missing the heartbeat of discipleship.

Sometimes, when I ask a person who is discipling them, they give the name of their pastor or an author. This is a red flag for me, signaling that real discipleship is not happening in this person's life. Perhaps a person is being discipled by their pastor through regular meetings and conversation. I know that does happen, but it does not happen often. To be clear, you cannot be discipled by a person who is not regularly in your life and speaking into your brokenness with love, truth, and light. And you definitely cannot be discipled by someone you have never met.[1] Personal relationship between the disciple and disciplemaker is non-negotiable.

To reengage the Great Commission, we must move beyond limiting discipleship to advanced spiritual disciplines, sermons, or small-group book studies. It's time to stop abdicating disciplemaking to a professional class of spiritual gurus and return to God's way of doing things.

God designed us to make disciples. Which means *disciplemaking is for anyone and everyone*. And more than that, *disciplemaking needs anyone and everyone*. Everyone has a part to play.

On an expedition, no one gets to coast through the journey. Everyone has responsibilities, no matter their skill level.

Look at those Jesus called to be his disciples and carry his message to the world. They came from diverse backgrounds and had different gifts and passions. Some were educated (Matthew and Judas Iscariot); some were not (Andrew, Peter, James, and John). They were from conflicting social factions and held different worldviews. Why did Jesus call such a diverse array of individuals to be his core Twelve? Perhaps it was, in part, to demonstrate that anyone can be a disciple and that anyone can be a disciplemaker.

The people who followed Jesus included men and women of every age and socioeconomic background, and very few religious leaders. Jesus' invitation was to ordinary people to

---

[1] I'm sure your favorite book or Bible study author would be flattered that you think they are discipling you, but you cannot disciple someone you don't know. You cannot hear God's will and word for someone specifically in that kind of relationship. Likewise, while the content in this book may be teaching you something, I am not discipling you either. I am, however, praying and interceding for you to answer the call of the Great Commission in general.

become his disciples and disciplemakers. We don't have to be an expert Christian to be a disciplemaker. The everyday person who feels lost and overwhelmed can be equipped and qualified.

Disciplemaker Pro Tip:

Often we try to teach people the algebra and calculus of disciplemaking, but most people just really need some good arithmetic. We need to keep disciplemaking simple and provide easy tools that even a baby Christian can wield. Churches all over the world are started by teenagers. If we believe a fifteen-year-old can make disciples, and we help equip her to do it, then any of us can do it.

Disciplemaking is not reserved for the mature, educated, "arrived," or confident. It is not simply for the elders, the leaders, or the clergy. It is not just the pastor's job, the missionary's job, the guest speaker's job, or the Bible study leader's job. It is everyone's job. God anoints us for specific assignments, but everyone who claims Jesus as Lord is called to make disciples.

If Jesus asked young John to be a disciplemaker, confident that with Holy Spirit's help, he could do it, then any young person can do the same. If Jesus handed over the "keys of the Kingdom" to Peter (Matthew 16:19, NLT), then any blue-collar Joe can be a disciplemaker. If Jesus can speak to a woman of a different ethnicity hiding in her shame (Samaritan woman at the well, John 4) and release her to become one of the first missionaries of his message, then any baby Christian can be released to make disciples.

Every person can be a disciplemaker, no matter how young in age or young in the faith. You only have to be a couple of steps ahead of a person to disciple them. A young adult can disciple a teen, a teen can disciple a middle-school kid, and a middle-school kid can disciple a child. A new Christian can disciple a newer Christian, and a baby Christian can disciple a person who has not yet believed. God is so good the way he made this all possible!

Jesus made discipleship the heartbeat of spreading the gospel. That's because without discipleship, without the passing on of the Good News from person to person to person, you end up with only one person telling one person at a time, a slow trickle that eventually slows to a stop. But if you take two people and they each disciple two people, who each go on to disciple two people—the growth is exponential. The movement of ordinary people answering the call is unstoppable.

The Disciple's Journey

As the afternoon sun dropped behind the rock wall, the group circled up. The first day of climbing was coming to an end. I asked people to share about a moment they had that day where they made the choice to trust something—whether that was the rope, the person belaying, or themselves. Several people had already shared when Lisa tentatively raised her hand. She was a nervous eighteen-year-old who had struggled but eventually succeeded that day on a couple of climbs.

"I had a moment I would like to share." Lisa looked down at her toes, her voice quiet. "On the first climb I got stuck and started getting scared. I prayed and asked God for help. And he answered me. He helped me be strong, and I made it. I think it was the first time God ever answered my prayer."

As I listened to Lisa, I thought about this young lady who had spent most of her life in church and yet had never experienced God answering her prayer. But God had met her where she could hear him clearly—out in the middle of the adventure we were on. And it had awakened her heart.

The disciple's journey begins with an ordinary person answering Jesus' call to follow him. In the New Testament, James and John were sitting in their father's boat, mending nets after a hard morning of fishing. As they wove the heavy thread together, a rabbi stopped to talk with them. He was cordial, considerate, and incredibly wise. There was something about this rabbi that was different. And then, suddenly, he invited James and John to follow him. So they did. They dropped their nets and left their father's boat to walk after him (Matthew 4:21-22).

Discipleship in the way of Jesus doesn't just involve a single decision—it is many daily decisions. Discipleship is a way of life. To follow Jesus, we commit to move and keep on moving into becoming more like Jesus.

I made my first decision to follow Jesus when I was three years old, but each time I come to a fork in the road of my life, each time God asks me to do something hard, I have to choose again to follow him. Making the daily choice to follow Jesus is not about salvation but about continually yielding to his version of my life's story and laying my own script down on the altar.

Being a disciple is not about acquiring information, but about being recreated and living out what we have learned. We are continually discovering who God is, who Jesus is, who Holy Spirit is, who we are, and how we are called to live and be in this world. Discipleship is also a quest of identity formation. It is God awakening our heart to his truth and his love, of us seeing ourselves in light of that new truth. It is repenting of any misunderstandings we have about God and being remade as new understanding becomes part of our identity. We die and are reborn in each season, in each trial, and ultimately in each day. The rhythm of trial and overcoming becomes the rhythm of baptism and rebirth. Each step gains us the prize of the character and nature of Christ.

In my own life, I have gone through the Hero's Journey cycle several times. Each season, my ordinary world has been challenged by its own call, a team to be a part of, and new things to learn. Each season has had its own lie of the enemy to overcome and its own unique breakthrough. Through them I have grown as a disciple of Jesus. And this is the journey every disciple is walking out—including you.

PERSONAL REFLECTION

Think about your life and journey with Jesus. How many cycles of the Hero's Journey do you see in your story? What were some things you learned in each one?

A Quest, Not a Ladder

Discipleship is not a ladder, or a set of blocks, that creates a stairway to maturity, heaven, or the next leadership position. That is not how people learn, grow, and change. Change happens when what you think you know is challenged—like when you came face-to-face with sin in your life and Jesus saved you, bringing resurrection power and restoration. Your ordinary life and story is exactly what God wants from you—that and the willingness to take the next step.

The life of faith is more like this video game I grew up playing: *The Legend of Zelda.* At the beginning of the game, you start out on a map covered in fog. You can't see anything at all. As you walk and explore, the fog recedes and you uncover new challenges. At each challenge you gain treasures that will help you win other challenges. And the further you go on your quest, the more the fog lifts and the map opens.

On the quest of discipleship, no person's story is the same. You often cannot see what is ahead. But the journey becomes clearer the further you go. This is why your story matters. There are places on the map you have explored, revelations that you have gained that others have not. And you get to share them. You walked the Hero's Journey of that season and now you get to be a hero maker, passing along the wisdom you learned.

If you have struggled, gained revelation, and now live changed by Jesus, you completed a cycle of your own Hero's Journey. Now Jesus calls you into a new cycle, further into the quest, helping others on the same adventure. This is how a disciple becomes a disciplemaker.

Jesus asks us to follow him into the unknown, beyond our own capacity and capability. Jesus calls us to die to self and pass on to others what we have received from our life with God.

In my opinion, God brilliantly "gamified"[2] discipleship from the beginning. God leads us in a way that motivates us to follow him. We chase his guidance, not knowing the full map or full story. As we go along, we overcome, find treasures, and uncover more mysteries. Sometimes we think God is playing hide-and-seek with us to test us. But really, he just wants us to pursue him into places we have never been.

The journey of discipleship is the ultimate adventure. Often we shy away from pain, struggle, and the call to grow, believing that comfort and security will bring us a fulfilled

---

[2] Anything that moves us without our conscious awareness is gamification.

life. But we don't magically "arrive"; we are not teleported to Christlikeness. We must journey there. We must take the long way around. Through the valleys and over the mountains, we learn each lesson with our own eyes and with our own two feet. Like worn leather boots, our soles tell the story of where we have been. Each cut, sap stain, or sun-faded patch is earned on the trail. As a journey shapes our shoes, the adventure of following Jesus shapes our hearts.

The path lies before you. Your backpack is already loaded. Jesus calls us all to follow in the footsteps of Peter and John—to be ordinary people who have spent time with Jesus and follow him on a grand quest as both a disciple and a disciplemaker. Will you answer that call? Will you join the adventure?

Discussion Questions

1. How have we made discipleship and disciplemaking complicated?

Download the Hero's Journey template at ordinarydiscipleship.com

2. What do you think about the idea that ordinary people are called to make disciples? How does it encourage you?

3. What concerns does this idea raise for you?

4. What kinds of people do you see Jesus recruiting to be disciplemakers?

5. What do you think about the idea that disciplemaking needs everyone? What kinds of people do you think are missing in our conversations and encouragement around making disciples (i.e. younger, older, people with disabilities)?

Inventory

At the beginning of the chapter, we looked at this Scripture passage:

> The members of the council were amazed when they saw the boldness of Peter and John, for they could see that they were ordinary men with no special training in the Scriptures. They also recognized them as men who had been with Jesus.
>
> ACTS 4:13, NLT

How does the Scripture speak to you now? What new meaning does it carry for you?

What revelations or insights are you taking away from this chapter? Capture them here:

Revelation/Insight #1

Revelation/Insight #2

LIVES CHANGED

EXPERIENCES REVELATION

LEARNS NEW THINGS

FEELS THE STRUGGLE

TEAMS WITH OTHERS

ANSWERS THE CALL

ORDINARY PERSON

DISCERNS THE SEASON

3

ANSWERS THE CALL

Joining the Cosmic Group Project

Hear, O Israel: The LORD our God, the LORD is one. Love the LORD your God with all your heart and with all your soul and with all your strength. These commandments that I give you today are to be on your hearts. Impress them on your children. Talk about them when you sit at home and when you walk along the road, when you lie down and when you get up. Tie them as symbols on your hands and bind them on your foreheads. Write them on the doorframes of your houses and on your gates.

DEUTERONOMY 6:4-9, NIV

I WATCHED ELIJAH'S WATER BOTTLE swing from his backpack as he hiked in front of me through the red dirt of the Grand Canyon. He was a little older and a lot taller than me, which meant his long legs ate up more trail with each stride. I had to hike at a slightly faster pace to keep up. It was the last day of our instructor training course, and I was excited for Elijah to be a part of the team. He was already a capable guide and had worked elsewhere, though past life choices left him feeling nervous and disqualified from being a spiritual mentor.

"I just don't know if I can do it. You guys are taking a big chance on me." His voice floated back to me over his shoulder as we hiked in the cooler morning air. I reflected on the past few days. We had arrived at our water source only to find it dried up. So we had to make a group decision whether to stretch out what we had or hike in the cooler parts of the day until we made it to our next water stop. Elijah had shown an ability to lead the group in asking and listening to Holy Spirit. I pointed out that he had just as much to offer as a spiritual leader as he did as a technical guide. Elijah had taken the teachable moment to heart, really allowing himself to be changed by repentance and prayer and embracing a different kind of leadership style. Like the rest of us, he was a work in progress, but his yielded heart was beautiful.

"I don't see it that way at all," I replied between breaths. "It is not about how you made choices then, but how you make decisions now. Think of all the people who can learn from your life. Think of all you have to share. You are in a humble, teachable place where you can both receive and give. I am always thrilled to work with people who are in that spot. God can do so much with them."

Elijah was quiet as he reflected on my words. I wondered if he had ever considered his weakness as an asset or his failures as treasures of revelation to share with others. And I hoped he would choose to stay.

The Call

We are called to an epic journey, a life that is full of adventure and challenge and abundance (John 10:10). The story will have some unforeseen plot twists, and the journey will take some unexpected turns. And yes, we'll experience suffering and anguish—alongside rejoicing and gloriousness—along the way. We have an enemy, a real antagonist who wants us to live diminished lives. But a disciple can live in the truth. We are created for boundless love; we are created to do amazing things; we are to share this journey with others.

At the end of Matthew's Gospel, Jesus gave what is known as the Great Commission:

> Then Jesus came to them and said, "All authority in heaven and on earth has been given to me. Therefore go and make disciples of all nations, baptizing them in the name of the Father and of the Son and of the Holy Spirit, and teaching them to obey everything I have commanded you. And surely I am with you always, to the very end of the age."
> MATTHEW 28:18-20, NIV

If you've heard this verse before, you probably have thought of it as a task or a command from Jesus. But it is actually an invitation to go adventuring with the Trinity—to see and do incredible things! The journey of being a disciple is the great quest for the light of Christ, the love of Christ, and the life of Christ in all that is around us. And we start the journey as a disciplemaker when we realize that God has called us not only to the adventure of our own life, but to share the adventure with others along the way. Just as Jesus sent out seventy-two disciples with only what they already had (Luke 10:1-4), disciplemaking is simply about journeying *with* someone to see them be changed by Jesus.

So let's invite others on the great exploration of an abundant life. In the Great Commission, Jesus does not tell us to *be* his disciples. He does not call us to obey everything he has commanded. Instead, he tells us to teach others to follow the commands. Maybe this is because he understands us well enough to know that we only really do something ourselves when we are trying to teach it to others.

I love how smart God is—how much he really gets human nature. He knows that our faith often grows and becomes more alive by giving to and discipling others. As we grow in embracing the fullness of life, we become better able to disciple others to do the same—and as we disciple others, we grow in our own experience of joy and adventure with God. The two spur each other on. Now, having discipled others successfully, I *hunger* to do it again. Not for the success, but for how God speaks to me and what *I* learn from the relationship.

The good news is that if you have embraced the journey of life in Christ, whether you see yourself as a hero or not, you can answer the call to be a disciplemaker. If you are sojourner following Jesus, you can be a friend and ally to those who are on their journey as well. And if you have learned anything from your time with Jesus, you have something to pass on to others.

Facing Our Fears

When you're about to rappel down the side of a cliff, there is this moment of transition as you step off the top. You kneel, holding the rope tightly down by your hip with one hand and up by your face with the other, and then you slowly lean back into the openness of space. This puts tension on the rope and equipment at your face. As you inch your feet downward, you continue to lean backward—a counterintuitive move when you're a hundred feet off the ground. In this moment of cosmic faith, your weight shifts from something you control (your legs) to something you are trusting in (ropes and equipment).

I have rappelled off a cliff at least a thousand times, but I still always experience butterflies when I make that transition. But every time, as I take that leap of faith, I am rewarded with the exhilaration of the descent. My reluctance to go over the edge is replaced with joy at being able to see and do things that only come from facing that fear.

As you contemplate this call to disciple another person, you probably are experiencing some butterflies and have a lot of questions. What makes a person ready to be a disciplemaker? Is it their level of experience, maturity, or title? If that were true, very few would qualify. Our adversary wants us to believe that we don't have what it takes. Since the moment Jesus gave the Great Commission, Satan has actively been working in people's lives and through the voices of others to disqualify us from being disciplemakers.

While something like moral failure can be a reason for disqualification from disciplemaking,[1] most people consider themselves disqualified because of the narratives in their own minds or in the systems of religion that say so. We hear

---

[1] Moral failure is a valid reason for disqualification, whether due to sexual or financial issues, rebellion, or abuse of power. But there is room and tremendous value in the process of real repentance, submission to consequences, and restoration. Indeed, some of the most effective disciplemakers I know stand on the other side of moral failure.

whispers in our head that we don't know enough of the Bible, that our life is not perfect enough, that we may make a mistake and say something wrong, that we are too shy or too young, or that we are just a simple person trying to go about our own life.

Historically the people of Jesus have wrestled with many charges of disqualification for disciplemaking:

- Wrong nationality
- Wrong family/lineage
- Wrong class
- Wrong race
- Not a property owner
- Wrong gender
- Wrong age
- Not enough experience
- Too much emotion in their spirituality
- Lack of presence of signs and miracles
- Lacking licensure or denominational approval
- Lacking title
- Lacking ordination
- Lacking education
- Past sin
- Current sin
- (Insert your failure or limit here.)

With such a list, who then could be qualified? But the great news is that it is not your own doubts, fears, or the world that decides if you are qualified—it is Jesus himself. If you love Jesus, then the Great Commission applies to you.

You are commissioned—you are called—you are qualified! And as with Elijah in the opening story, sometimes it is our past failures that God wants to use to help others. If God could take the apostle Paul, who harassed and persecuted the church, and use him as an instrument to spread the message of grace to the known world, then he can use your story as well.

PERSONAL REFLECTION

What in your life has been used against you to make you feel disqualified from being a disciplemaker?

Therefore, there is now no condemnation for those who are in Christ Jesus.
ROMANS 8:1, NIV

You can see each part of your story either as an obstacle to overcome, or as an opportunity from God to help you uncover treasures he wants you to pass on to others. Your lessons, revelations, and breakthroughs are as much for the disciple-making of others as they are for your own growth. You can't control what you've been handed, but you can control what you do with it.

And your company of travelers awaits. Yes, there are people waiting for you to answer this call. People who *need* you to answer this call—because something about who you are and how you relate to God speaks to who they are and how God relates to them.

Passing It On

Throughout Scripture, we see how God's work in one person's life meets the needs of someone else. Take Moses and Joshua, for example. Moses started mentoring Joshua when Joshua was a young man. Moses likely got to know him while they were dealing with Pharaoh in Egypt, because the first time that we see Joshua in Scripture, he is already leading others into battle (Exodus 17:8-16). From then on, we read that Joshua is often with Moses, doing things with him as the Israelites traveled in the wilderness.

While Moses may have sat down regularly with Joshua and "taught" him, Scripture does not mention it. Instead, we read in Exodus 33:11 that Moses took Joshua *with him* when he met face to face with God. Moses' approach as a guide/mentor looked less like school learning and more like experiential learning.[2] As Moses walked his own Hero's Journey, he invited Joshua to be a part of it.

Joshua had his friends and peers, like Caleb, but he walked with Moses and learned from him on his good days and on his bad days. Moses was his ally, his cheerleader, his mentor.

Just as Joshua took over leadership of the Israelites after Moses and led them where Moses could not, each of us is meant to raise up the next generation to go further than we do. Our ceiling is meant to be their platform. They are supposed to accomplish what we cannot.[3]

Perhaps your passions are meant to inspire and prepare others for their calling. As we read of the heroes of the faith in Hebrews,

---

[2] For example, see Exodus 17:8-16; Exodus 24:13; Exodus 32:17-19; and Exodus 33:11.

[3] The next generation should stand on our shoulders, not our graves.

> These were all commended for their faith, yet none
> of them received what had been promised, since God
> had planned something better for us so that only
> together with us would they be made perfect.
>
> HEBREWS 11:39-40, NIV

The whole point of faith and life in God is making disciples and raising up the next generation of faithful followers. Moses had his Hero's Journey, but he did not get to see all that God had promised. He needed those who came after him to take the next step. He needed to disciple someone to pick up where he left off.

But Moses did not just need Joshua to pick up the next leg of the journey. Hebrews 11:40 makes it clear that all the heroes described in Hebrews need *us* to continue forward into the ongoing fulfillment of God's promises. In that sense, Moses' and Joshua's Hero's Journeys are not complete without your Hero's Journey. And your Hero's Journey is not complete without the journey of those whom you disciple.

No one understood this better than Jesus himself. If anyone could have been a lone-ranger hero, Jesus could have. He had all the power in the universe, and yet he specifically chose not to go it alone. More than once Jesus filled large venues with people anxious to hear him speak, like on a hillside or by the Sea of Galilee. But his messages were challenging and hard to take. People did not necessarily walk away feeling better about themselves.

Jesus could have gone all "big stage," preaching inspiring messages and setting up a movement that would have made him a political king.[4] But instead, he made the counterintuitive

---

4 Jesus could have inspired revolt and thrown out the Roman Empire, giving the land of Israel back to the Jewish people to rule.

decision to intensely invest in a few people. Jesus chose to go small and deep rather than big and broad.

Instead of having an event-only method of ministry, Jesus modeled, explained, and spoke to groups both big and small along the way. Jesus created opportunities for others to try new things, and gave them the opportunity to make mistakes. The twelve disciples often got things wrong! Remember Peter? He made mistakes all the time. Peter wanted to build tents when it was time to go, sleep when it was time to pray, lead when it was time to follow, and follow when it was time to lead.

We are fond of Peter because his struggles give us hope. We can identify with his sincere clumsiness. I personally resonate with Peter's tendency to leap first and ask questions later.[5] If Jesus can look at Peter and find him worthy of passing on the Good News, then that means Jesus looks at you and me and all our flaws and failures and finds us worthy too. If Jesus could return to heaven, confident in Peter and Holy Spirit to make disciples, then perhaps we can find a way to believe that Jesus has confidence in our ability to make disciples also.

Jesus worked with Peter and the other disciples to place in them the treasure of a deep relationship with the Father and eyes to see the Kingdom. These experiences with Jesus, the Son of the God of the universe, became the treasures that the disciples passed along to others. It was that simple. Jesus called people to teach others what had been revealed to them personally. And Jesus' call in the Great Commission is the same to us today.

---

[5] This has gotten me in trouble more than once. My husband often says that my enthusiasm is unencumbered by reality.

PERSONAL REFLECTION

How do the examples from Scripture give you hope? Are there any specific examples that encourage you?

Forged, Not Photocopied

Have you ever known someone who had the equipment to do something, like skiing, but never really went skiing? They could go anytime, but the skis just sat in the garage or basement collecting dust.

When you want to answer the call to adventure, just having the equipment is not enough; you also need to know how to use it. Sometimes guiding is simply about teaching people to use what they already have. Sometimes disciplemaking is like that too.

In my experience, disciplemaking is about everyday life, equipping people in the ways of Jesus, and empowering them to live as missionaries in every space where they walk. Most people do not see themselves accurately. You get to join Jesus in being a cheerleader for others, reminding people of who the Bible says they are, what God is calling them to, and how Holy Spirit is there to help them in everything. You get to help someone else connect what they are going through with what God says about them. This is why learning is a relational process. The relationship between the disciple and disciplemaker is what Holy Spirit uses as the path for shaping and development. What an amazing way to be used by God!

In his fantastic book *The Divine Conspiracy*, Dallas Willard

Disciplemaker Pro Tip:

Is there anyone in your everyday life that you sense the Lord is drawing you toward to care about and pray for? Do you notice the Lord also drawing them toward you? Do they ask you for wisdom or advice and respond positively to you? Pray about whether God wants to continue to draw you closer to each other and whether you are to have more of a peer relationship (like Peter and Paul) or a disciple/disciplemaker relationship (like Paul and Timothy). The relationship can be formal (you regularly meet to have conversations) or informal (you listen for teachable moments in casual conversation and water what God is already doing).

says that the goal of discipleship is "to live my life as [Jesus] would live my life if he were I."[6] In other words, our goal is not to make people (or to become ourselves) exact copies of Jesus. Instead, Christ is formed *in* us, which is why the purpose of being a disciple is "allowing Jesus to live his life through us." We want Jesus to remake us from the inside out, so that our character and nature, lived out through our unique personality and circumstances, becomes the same as Jesus' character and nature.

The difference is subtle yet important. In a Western culture, people believe we are shaped by outside forces, as though we are an object, a widget—like a piece of marble worn down and carved into a replica image by the sculptor's hands. The problem is that while the marble looks like the person into whose image it was carved, it never takes on the nature of the person. It can never be anything but marble. This is not what it means, as the

---

6 Dallas Willard, *The Divine Conspiracy* (San Francisco: HarperSanFrancisco, 1998), 283.

apostle Paul puts it, to be "conformed to the image of [Christ]" (Romans 8:29, NIV).

Instead, Peter talks about the refining fire of the Lord (1 Peter 1:7). Have you ever seen iron being forged? It is quite a process. The fire must be over 2000 degrees Fahrenheit. The metal is heated and flattened and folded back upon itself like dough, then molded together again. The process of heating, tamping, and cooling doesn't just change the shape, it also changes the hardness of the metal, making it stronger and more durable. The very nature of the iron is changed as it is heated and hammered.

What sounds like a brutal process is actually quite precise. Make the metal too hot or try to fold it too many times and the whole thing can fall apart. Iron is not a hard object to be pounded into a form, but an object to be made soft, melted, and molded into whatever the master craftsman desires. A sword is formed from the inside out, not something carved from the outside in.

We are not meant to be a photocopy of Jesus, which would never be mistaken for the real person. Instead, through discipleship, our inside nature—our very essence—is transformed. Like iron transformed into steel, we are refined and changed into the nature of Jesus. Jesus is formed inside of us, walking around with *our* faces and *our* hands and *our* hearts. And as that happens, we live our unique adventure in a way that reminds others of Jesus.

This is the journey the disciplemaker encourages the disciple to take, helping them discern within the context of their life and circumstances. It is the disciplemaker who bears witness to the change process, affirming and celebrating the transformation.

PERSONAL REFLECTION

How have you previously thought about being conformed to the image of Christ? How do you think about that now?

The Disciplemaking Disciple

In my twenties, I was fortunate that the outdoor community I was part of also believed deeply in discipleship. I was just out of college, wet behind the ears, and working in full-time ministry. There were so many things I did not know, and even more questions I did not even know to ask. But I was surrounded by people who loved Jesus and simply tried to put into practice the things he said.

When I first joined the community and expressed the desire to be discipled, the other women discussed among themselves which one would meet with me regularly. Collectively, they all discipled me.[7] But while they all embraced a level of responsibility for my spiritual formation, it was Diana who met with me on a routine basis.

We'd sit down over lunch or coffee, and Diana would ask me questions about my life. She would share about her life and what God was teaching her. She modeled what following Jesus looked like and discussed with me how I followed Jesus. She also asked me about the people I was discipling, processing with me how I was teaching them to be disciplemakers. At any one time, the disciplemaking chain had an average of five links, with Diana and me making up the middle.

---

[7] We talk more about the community aspects of discipleship in the next chapter.

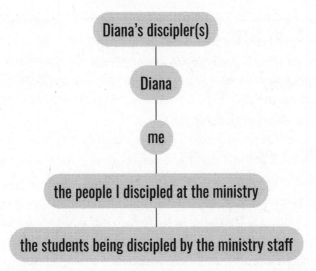

In the ministry I helped lead, I oversaw the in-depth discipleship of about four thousand different people. I intentionally discipled about a hundred people through relationships, and I apprenticed about two dozen people in full-time ministry.[8] But I was able to do this only because I was first brought into a community that valued discipleship, where each person took responsibility for the spiritual maturation of someone else.

The idea of coaching, mentoring, or supporting someone else in their own life as a disciple can be a little scary. It causes us to stop and take stock of who we are and what resources we have. One of the foundational truths of disciplemaking is that we can't give what we don't have and that we can only reproduce who we are. To be a disciplemaker, we must first be a disciple ourselves.

Each disciplemaker is still in process (of course!) and still

---

[8] Not singularly, but as a co-leader and co-laborer.

makes mistakes. That's why it's vital for each disciplemaker to also be a disciple. They have someone in their life to help guide and correct them. Each misstep becomes a teachable moment. This was true for me. It kept me from some missteps, helped me reduce the damage of others, and helped my heart heal after I screwed something up.

A guide improves when they are with others who mentor and push them. If we are not in a discipleship relationship with someone who pours into us, we model for others that relationship is not necessary and that faith is a private, independent matter. This says we believe that discipleship is only for the new or immature Christian and not necessary for us to fulfill our life of faith. It demonstrates that we do not think discipleship is vital for the Christian walk and Kingdom life.

The longer I worked as a guide, the more joy I found in learning from others—their revelations, their tricks, their experiences. Their wisdom inspired me and reminded me I was not alone. God's heart is not that we would graduate from "discipleship school," but rather that we become more desperate and more dependent upon the Cross and the work of Holy Spirit in our lives. Personally, each season with the Lord has only served to increase my own need for discipleship, for mentors and peers to walk with me on this amazing journey. They remind me that this path is both new and known. They point me to others who came before and have insights to share, while at the same time being present with me in the freshness of my experience.

Great discipleship relationships feed our soul, move us forward on the path, and shape our life with God. None of us has a complete revelation of God and the mystery of the work of Jesus. We know this, and God knows this too. You never "arrive" and then share—you share along the way. Peter said, "Silver or gold I do not have, but what I do have I give you" (Acts 3:6, NIV). Your lack is not a reason to avoid making disciples! God knows exactly who you are and what you have, which is why he called you in the first place.

Contemplating the call to be a disciplemaker is no small thing. I believe God gets excited when we say, "Okay, I will do this big, crazy thing, but I am limited, and I need you to be God and do most of it." Believing in ourselves enough to take a step is a type of faith that gives glory to God.

Discussion Questions

1. Reflect on your process of continuously being transformed into the image of Christ. Was this journey more from the outside in or the inside out?

2. Why do you think that many discipleship processes are from the outside in?

3. How do we as a community create value around the idea of never graduating from being a disciple?

4. What are some of your internal fears and objections— reasons in your mind—about why you should not be a disciplemaker?

5. Consider the discipleship chain with each person investing in the life of someone just a little bit behind them on life's path. What benefits do you see in this strategy? What concerns you? How can you address those concerns without returning to what doesn't work?

Inventory

At the beginning of the chapter, we looked at this Scripture passage:

> Hear, O Israel: The LORD our God, the LORD is one. Love the LORD your God with all your heart and with all your soul and with all your strength. These commandments that I give you today are to be on your hearts. Impress them on your children. Talk about them when you sit at home and when you walk along the road, when you lie down and when you get up. Tie them as symbols on your hands and bind them on your foreheads. Write them on the doorframes of your houses and on your gates.
> DEUTERONOMY 6:4-9, NIV

How does the Scripture sound to you now? What new meaning does it carry for you?

What revelations or insights are you taking away from this chapter? Capture them here:

Revelation/Insight #1

Revelation/Insight #2

LIVES CHANGED

EXPERIENCES REVELATION

LEARNS NEW THINGS

FEELS THE STRUGGLE

TEAMS WITH OTHERS

ANSWERS THE CALL

ORDINARY PERSON

DISCERNS THE SEASON

4

TEAMS WITH OTHERS

The Community of Tables, Ropes, and Campfires

*Dear, dear Corinthians, I can't tell you how much I long for
you to enter this wide-open, spacious life. We didn't fence
you in. The smallness you feel comes from within you. Your
lives aren't small, but you're living them in a small way. I'm
speaking as plainly as I can and with great affection. Open
up your lives. Live openly and expansively!*

2 CORINTHIANS 6:11-13, MSG

"HEY!" WE CALLED OUT as we walked in the door of Joe[1] and
Alison Arnold's house, carrying side dishes and folding chairs.
My husband took the Crock-Pot to the kitchen, while I took
the folding chairs to the large open painting studio. As usual,
what was planned as a "small Thanksgiving gathering" had
grown to more than forty people. Surrounding the long table
in the studio were vinyl and chrome 1950s kitchen chairs,
a couple 1930s wooden armchairs with fraying jacquard
upholstery, aluminum folding chairs, mid-century American

---

[1] Drew Arnold (chapter 1) and Joe were brothers. They planted a church together
and started SROM together.

oak chairs, and a wooden bench. I added my black plastic folding chairs to the eclectic collection.

A chair was conspicuously missing at the head of the table. This place, we all knew, was reserved for Drew Arnold and his wheelchair, so he could serve as master of ceremonies, his favorite role. Drew steered the motorized chair to his place and welcomed everyone. As we passed around food, Drew shared about the first Thanksgiving. With skilled storytelling he described how the Native Americans helped save the surviving Mayflower immigrants by teaching them how to farm in the New World.

Thanksgiving was a celebration of their first successful harvest, the sign that they would survive the upcoming winter.

"We are here today because of the kindness of strangers," Drew reminded us. I looked around the room. The menagerie of chairs matched the faces of those seated at the table: family, friends, international students from the university, and people met during the week who had "no plans" for the holiday. Sharing the table were the orphan, the widow, and the foreigner. Many of us had been invited into the Arnolds' life as strangers, but what we found was belonging.

Pull Up a Chair

When Lily came on one of our wilderness trips, she had been feeling isolated in her life of faith for a long time. She had been raised in a Christian community that cared more about performance as a Christian than her relationship with God. Scripture was quoted *at* her instead of read *with* her, and she often felt lectured by her leaders. Lily had followed God's leading to come on a wilderness course so she could "figure out how to get her life together."

One afternoon on the expedition, while struggling to climb a rocky slope, she slipped and scraped up her leg. As she sat down to deal with her wound and her fear, another student came and sat with her. Another grabbed her pack to carry it up the slope in addition to their own. It was the first time Lily had found herself surrounded by others in her struggle. Previously, she had to face things alone, but this time someone else came along beside her to help and encourage her. That moment—that first taste of belonging—transformed her life.

None of us are meant to travel our journey alone. Foundationally, discipleship is a community endeavor. You cannot disciple yourself. Literally, it takes two people! We are meant to come alongside others, and we are meant to accept help and let others lead us. Interdependence is fundamental to the life of faith. When an ordinary person answers the call to the adventure of discipleship, they discover people who are on the same journey (friends, allies, mentors) and connect with them. There are no solo heroes in the Kingdom of God.

And it doesn't have to be complicated. Often, we think of disciplemaking as some form of school or ministry preparation, recalling Sunday school teachers, youth leaders, or pastors who have discipled us. But when we reflect, we can usually think of others who have shaped our understanding of God or who modeled what it means to be a Christian in practical ways. I think of the elderly woman across the street who hosted a half-day VBS at her house for the neighborhood kids when I was growing up. She would quiz me about Bible stories while I ate her chocolate chip cookies. Or there's the friend of mine who worked at the post office and always thought of himself as a missionary in his workplace. He was known for bringing people joy.

Both the woman across the street and my post-office friend were living the same way as our little Thanksgiving crowd: inviting others in and giving them a seat at the Kingdom table, no matter how mismatched their chair was.

God intended all of us to be disciplemakers. We can each set up a table and invite someone to pull up a chair. We don't have to make it complicated.

Spiritual transformation is challenging, but it is not complex. There is a King and his Kingdom, and we are created to fellowship there as brothers and sisters. We are students, apprentices, and practitioners of the ways of Jesus. We are obedient to what God is saying, and we respond with faith. We do all this with the guidance and prompting of Holy Spirit (1 Corinthians 2:10; John 14:26; John 16:13). The process of transformation happens through learning and unlearning, relationship, and imitation, which is why we need others.

As disciplemakers, we walk in close relationship with those we disciple, but our relationship is not *just a* friendship. A guide can enjoy the company of those they are leading, but they must be more than friends. They also have to help equip others. As disciplemakers, we have a simple, God-given agenda—transformation. We hope, pray, contend, intercede, and intentionally guide the disciple to be more like Jesus.

Formation, as evidenced by transformation, is the purpose of discipleship. As a disciplemaker we must explore two questions:

- How do formation and transformation happen in ourselves?
- How can we encourage these things in others?

While we will spend the next two chapters exploring these questions, right now we're going to spend some time looking specifically at the role relationships play, namely that connection to our brothers and sisters is both the means *and* the content of discipleship.

Relationships are the key to authentic discipleship. No longer are we disconnected strangers living in different houses. Instead, we are connected sojourners on an epic expedition together. It makes all the difference in the world. People grow in their relationship with God by observing and learning from those around them—those who are further on in their journey. We are increasingly transformed by being together.

PERSONAL REFLECTION

Who has helped you grow in your connection with God? How did that happen—(for example, in a church, through a discipleship class, in a family context, in a friendship)? Who in your life has served as a guide and a mentor, encouraging you, shaping you, and asking you questions? What did you learn from them?

Roped Up!

I took my first fall on a mountain snow slope when I was seven years old. My dad and I were climbing South Teton—a big deal for a tiny kid. Located in Grand Teton National Park, the Tetons are picturesque mountains that jut seven thousand feet straight up above the valley floor. As we crossed the angled snowfield on the side of South Teton, a fall suddenly sent me sliding down the face of the mountain. Fortunately, I had my ice axe, and I was connected to my father with a rope. I easily stopped, climbed back up to where he waited, and continued on to the summit.

About fifteen years later, on Middle Teton, I was again climbing with my father when I took another fall. We were coming down from the summit through a section that included both rock and snow when the ice I was standing on broke. Suddenly I found myself sliding—down, down, about two hundred feet, instinctively chopping at the rock and snow with my ice axe. Not far beyond me, at the end of that slide, was over two thousand feet of sheer vertical space. Only by a miracle did my ice axe catch before I fell to my death.

In my first fall, I was connected by the rope to my dad, and everything was fine. But in my second fall, due to a series of poor decisions, I was not on belay and nearly fell to my death while my dad could only watch. I was not roped up . . . and it nearly cost me my life. The difference between the two falls wasn't just what equipment I was using, but how I thought about climbing. When I was seven years old, I knew I needed to take precautions. By the time I was twenty-two, I had a lot more experience and didn't think I could fall—so I didn't think about being connected to my climbing partners.

Paul talks about something like this in 1 Corinthians 10:12, where he reminds us that anyone can fall. That's why we need Jesus, and we need each other.

Every disciple needs to connect to a team and community. In climbing, we call this being "on belay"—one person supports the other with the help of a rope. Whether we are walking or climbing, if someone has shouted, "You are on belay!" then we know we are supported in our trek forward, beyond our comfort level, and possibly beyond our skill level. A disciplemaker needs to fill this role and stay connected to the disciple so they can keep going further.

So how can we harness the power of relationships for effective discipleship, partnering with God in the process of seeing Jesus change a disciple's life? I am a strong believer in being up front with people about what the disciplemaking relationship looks like:

- committed and covenantal
- encouraging and challenging
- authentic and transparent
- modeling and mirroring

Committed and Covenantal

Jesus came so that the Trinity could be in the middle of life's challenges with us. Some of us may have become a Christian simply because we were searching for more in life, or maybe because we were afraid of what would happen if we didn't choose God. But God wants so much more for us than to simply save us from our sins. He wants to abide with us now *and* on the other side of eternity.

God offers us more than just a life bartering with him in prayers and tithes, or serving in ministry so we can have a better life or get something specific in return. That's a transactional relationship—something a consumer does. But God has committed himself to us in a different way—through a covenantal and unbreakable promise.

This covenant is one of the ways we bear his image and experience the Kingdom as we journey together with others. We are called to connect to one another the same way God connects with us. Can you truly engage a communal adventure as a consumer? No. Strangers may climb on the same mountain, be friendly, even hike together, but they don't tie themselves together with a rope. That mutual support is a different level of commitment, one that God calls us to as team members in the Kingdom. God intends for us to belay one another, catching each other if we fall. And ultimately, when someone falls, we're not left holding the rope alone. God has all of us.

The twelve disciples understood this covenantal relationship. They committed to follow Jesus even when they did not like where they were going. Following Jesus involved sacrifice in their personal lives. They imposed upon one another and inconvenienced each other. They frustrated each other. It got messy. And even when they did abandon Jesus after his arrest (all except John), Jesus did not accept their rejection. Jesus chose to bind himself to the disciples, and after the Resurrection, the disciples reciprocated, binding themselves to back him and one another.

Transactional relationships are clean and can be severed at any time. They are designed for mutual control and can be broken by either party. Discipleship is much more interdependent. We rely on each other to make it through the climb. If we are to experience the richness of all that Jesus

died to give us, we have to move from transactional relationships to covenantal ones. We must have committed, non-
breaking bonds with one another. We need to be brave and
tie into the rope together.

PERSONAL REFLECTION

1. Think about your relationships with others. Which
    ones would you describe as more transactional?
    Which ones are more covenantal?
2. How is your relationship with God transactional? How
    is it covenantal?

Encouraging and Challenging

Russell was nervous, unsure, and shaky. I was belaying him
on his first rock climb, and Russell would climb up a step or
two and then stop, wanting to quit. But I would not let him.
"You can do this! You can go at least one more step. On
the right there is a bomber[2] foothold. You step on that and
you're golden!" I didn't want to let Russell down, because I
knew he was capable of more. With this truth in mind, Russell
would successfully make the next step, and I would continue
encouraging him. "Wow, look at that! You got this! You are
so close to the top now—don't quit. You got this. You can
make it!" Though I am very sure my relentless encouragement was annoying, Russell made it to the top, where he

---

2 *Bomber* means "really good." Climber slang is full of colorful adjectives and inspiring
expressions for all things positive and challenging. I think disciplemaking could
benefit from similar color commentary. Something like "That last season with Jesus
was epic!" or "The truth in that verse is so bomber, you could anchor off it!"

could enjoy the pride that comes from not giving up and achieving a goal.

Every authentic team or fellowship doing life together needs healthy relationship dynamics, and a good discipling relationship relies on getting the right balance of pushing and support. Jesus both encouraged and challenged his disciples, always in the context of love. A loving parent encourages and affirms their child in the things they do well but also challenges them in the areas in which they need to grow.

Transformation happens when someone is challenged to grow within the context of a loving and secure relationship. A person who never receives any challenge can quickly become complacent, and their growth can become stunted. On the other hand, someone who receives only challenge, with little encouragement, can quickly become discouraged. A healthy discipling relationship embraces both truth and love.

Holy Spirit is always gentle and kind (James 3:17), so even when we bring challenge to someone, it should always be coupled with kindness and humility. Knowing *how to* say something is as important as knowing *when to* say it. Sometimes people need a whisper, and sometimes they need something more direct, like a yell as they climb the

Disciplemaker Pro Tip:

We should not call out every issue we see. Sometimes the most obvious sin is not the one God wants to address first. Sometimes God is doing a deeper work in a place that is unseen. Our words need to reflect not only God's will, but also God's heart and God's tone—and they need to be said in God's timing.

rock face to "keep going." God knows what kind of communication our souls need at any one moment.

Once I discipled a person who was not very kind to their spouse. They were either rude or dismissive to them, but the Lord never gave me permission to speak to them about the situation. Instead, I was led to speak to them about their deep fear of rejection and how they acted out with controlling behavior when they were scared.

As disciplemakers, we need to be in tune with Holy Spirit and make sure our tone matches. Otherwise our words will not resonate and bring life. God is always doing something; we simply join him in it.

PERSONAL REFLECTION

We each have a default—encouragement or challenge. Which do you gravitate toward? How can you let Jesus guide you into a balanced voice? What strategies can you use to help make sure you are speaking only the way the Lord wants you to?

Authentic and Transparent

Fellowships are formed when life gets real. That is why camping is so good for bonding. Nothing is as real as seeing each other in the morning—morning breath, morning hair, pre-coffee grumpiness, and all. When we see others in the reality of who they are, we become more transparent ourselves. And there is nothing more bonding than sitting around a campfire.

Campfires are places where stories are told. Staring into the dancing flames as the opaque darkness sets in, we find the courage to open our souls. We drop our walls and our protections and open our lives.

Transactional relationships are not strong enough for real-life authenticity. To be a transformational disciplemaker, you must cultivate authenticity and transparency in the discipleship relationship. All of life needs to be on the table—both for you and for the person being discipled. If the purpose of discipleship is to help us give Jesus increasing lordship over our lives, then the disciplemaker needs to see and have permission to speak into the disciple's life. The disciple needs to choose to yield to the process.

This idea may sound anywhere from mildly scary to terrifying. No one is presentable at all times. There are parts of our lives we want to hide, thoughts we don't want to voice, ugliness in our souls we don't want anyone to see. That's why the discipling relationship must be built on trust and led by Holy Spirit. As a disciplemaker, we are constantly asking the Lord to lead us in what to speak to and what to leave unaddressed until he says otherwise.

To foster healthy transparency, I like to ask God to give me his heart for those I'm discipling. How does he view that person? What attributes does he love? How does he want to encourage them to do more? What piece of his image do they carry that the rest of the world needs to see? I also ask for compassion for the things that are less lovely to look at. As Christ followers, we are not supposed to be afraid of sin, because we understand that Jesus paid the price for it on the cross. As a disciplemaker, this must be all the more true. We need to create a safe space that allows people to be real.

We disciple in the way of Jesus when we live life openly. If we don't allow people to come close, the relational distance can unintentionally become a form of control and can create an unhealthy power difference between the disciple and the disciplemaker. To keep from creating power issues in the disciple/disciplemaker relationship, we must look to the standard—Jesus. The disciple/disciplemaker relationship should never be used or twisted to look different from the relationship Jesus had with his disciples.[3]

PERSONAL REFLECTION

Take a moment and think about the people around you. Who is God drawing you toward? Ask him for eyes to see that person as he sees them. Write down their names and ask Holy Spirit to direct how you should pray for them.

Modeling and Mirroring

When I teach a person to tie into a rope, I stand with them and model it for them. Each of us holds a piece of rope and I walk them through tying the knot so they can both watch me and copy me at the same time. This is how God designed us to learn best.

---

[3] Jesus lived life with his disciples, but he did draw away and have alone time, so this is not to suggest there is no veil between the disciple and disciplemaker. But modeling is a far better teacher than telling, and whatever veils exist between you and the person you are discipling should be intentional, agreed upon, and as thin as maturity allows.

This phenomenon, known as "mirroring," is just one of the many incredible ways we are fearfully and wonderfully made. A baby learns how to smile by looking at the faces of those who hold them. As an adult holds the baby and smiles, the adult's brain activates a certain pattern of muscle movements and emotions, such as happiness. When the baby sees the smile, the baby's brain "mirrors" the pattern of muscle movements and positive emotions. That mirrored activation pattern teaches the baby's face how to smile. As the baby's smile triggers the adult to smile, the process reinforces itself. How does the brain know to do this? It is one of God's fantastic mysteries.[4]

By looking at God, we mirror God and become more like him. This is the great purpose of mirroring. Living with unveiled faces (2 Corinthians 3:18) allows us to be transformed into the image of God. And when we live transparently before others, we also reflect the glory of God. As disciplemakers we are living examples, modeling what we want the disciples to learn. We model peace so they can mirror peace. We model joy so they can experience joy. We model a deep and intimate walk with God so they learn contentment in Christ.

You may be able to instruct others effectively, but it is *who you are* that has the greatest impact. Don't ignore the power of mirroring. Leverage it to help the person you disciple not just "practice what you preach" but "mirror who you are."

Life on Life

More than once I have been on a climb with my dad where we could not see or hear each other. Being roped together, the

---

[4] Cool nerd fact: Mirroring is why yawns are contagious.

only way we had to communicate was through rope signals and footprints. But being connected was enough to help me follow him.

Disciplemaking is more than inviting people into our lives to discuss topics or concepts from a book. It is not just about our prayer life or Scripture reading. It is much more vulnerable and transparent than that. The challenge of disciplemaking is allowing others into our lives to walk alongside us, encouraging them to "imitate me, just as I imitate Christ" (1 Corinthians 11:1, NLT). That's why many people call this "life-on-life" disciplemaking.

Being a disciple of Jesus isn't only about our behavior, but also about how we see ourselves. It is about how we see and treat others, and where our faith lies regarding delicate issues like finances or sexuality. It is about who we are at work and who we are with our families. All of life is on the table with Jesus, so life-on-life disciplemaking is about inviting people into all your life.

If people don't see your challenges, they won't understand your victories. If they don't see the struggle, they won't understand the overcoming. If they don't see what following Jesus looks like in difficult situations, they will think that tough times are a sign of failure. To disciple someone, you must let them see you—all of you—so they can see Jesus in you. Jesus laughed, cried, and was broken in front of his disciples. To be a disciplemaker like Jesus, you need to find the courage to do the same.

We need to share the dinner table, the moments of celebration, the moments of hardship, and the nondescript moments of everyday life with those we disciple. Have the disciple over to your home to spend time with your family. Let them see how you manage conflict in a healthy way. Let the everyday rhythms of your life show them *how* to be a follower of Jesus Monday through Sunday.

We are not trying to demonstrate perfection. Perfection and performance keeps people at a distance. Living transparently lets other people in. Modeling how to be a disciple-in-process is what's most valuable to others. Let Jesus show us what perfection looks like. The rest of us are just on a journey.

PERSONAL REFLECTION

What concerns do you have about discipling life-on-life? What parts of your life do you find hard to share? Why? What does God say about it all?

Share the Load

I discipled Aurora for a handful of years, through her dating, engagement, and early marriage years. But when she started to have a family, I was no longer the best person to provide the wisdom she needed. Not being able to have children myself, I realized that Aurora needed to meet regularly with others who better understood the challenges of her new season.

As a disciplemaker, we do not hold in our grasp all the experiences or wisdom a person needs to make it through complex seasons, nor are we able to mine the lessons of seasons we have not been through. When we accept this, we learn to see ourselves less as experts and more as seasonal guides who partner with the rest of the body of Christ. And that creates space for others to come around a disciple as well. When multiple people pour into a disciple, their strengths and weaknesses can complement each other. Because discipleship is holistic, it is also fundamentally a community activity, and we get to share the load with others.

Organizational research tells us that the maximum number of individuals a single person can sustainably influence at a life-on-life level is five.[5] I think about that a lot as a disciplemaker. *Five.* It is true that Jesus discipled twelve people. But there are considerations to take into account:

1. Jesus did this full time. (The Scriptures do not mention that he worked his trade during the time he was discipling.)
2. Jesus did not have family (wife, children, extended family) that the Bible mentions he took care of or earned income for.
3. Jesus was in an unbroken relationship with the Father and Holy Spirit.

Given the amount of time and focus Jesus could give to his earthly ministry, it makes sense that he could disciple more than five people in-depth. But as an experienced disciplemaker, with a family and job, I have found it difficult to life-on-life disciple more than three people at a time. Drew Arnold taught me that you can either have a shallow influence on a lot of people or a profound influence on a few. The choice is yours to make.

---

5 The one-to-five ratio comes from the book *Good to Great*, which says a great manager can at most handle five direct reports. There is other organizational research to support this as well. Discipleship, when done properly and holistically, is on par with being a good manager in terms of time, attention, and support.

The one-to-five ratio is not a limitation; it is an opportunity. If one person can *at most* disciple five people deeply, how do we disciple a small group, a church, or a town? We do it the way God intended—as a community. We can't do it all, and God doesn't require us to. We each can do only a little. God's desire and intention is that each believer plays their part, according to the seasons, and that together the community disciples the community. The pattern looks like this: journey, multiply, journey, multiply. It's cycle after cycle of the Hero's Journey.

Discipling people as a community also helps keep the disciple/disciplemaker relationship healthy, because it avoids potential overattachment with one particular individual. As disciples, we should have multiple voices in our lives that, together, help us to become more Christlike.

We are not meant to be individual spiritual gurus or build our own kingdoms of little disciples. Rather, in healthy discipleship, people are connected to one another through multiple avenues of life-giving relationships. All the people of the community take responsibility for building up and discipling one another, and together the community creates a discipleship culture.

PERSONAL REFLECTION

Think about a season of your life when you felt particularly invested in by those around you. What were the names and faces of those people whose influence and discipleship overlapped?

Swapping Leads

When we begin to see discipleship as a holistic, community activity, we come to see that an authentic discipleship relationship is a two-way relationship. Discipleship among followers of Jesus is never meant to be a one-way, authoritative relationship. The Bible says we are to call no one Rabbi but Jesus (Matthew 23:8). Rather, we and those we disciple become learners and sojourners who follow Jesus together.

With this said, the disciple/disciplemaker relationship is not necessarily an equal interaction, where there is an equal give-and-take into each other's lives. That dynamic is only found in peer relationships where "iron sharpens iron" (Proverbs 27:17). In a healthy disciple/disciplemaker relationship, we recognize that each may be in a different place of maturity, and so we bring a spirit of mutual submission to the person of Christ and the work of Holy Spirit in each other (Ephesians 5:21). Understanding differences in maturity is the key to Christian relationships and is more useful than rules.

Drew Arnold, who cultivated such a rich disciplemaking community, created the kind of culture in which all could learn from one another. He put PhDs and college freshmen, businesspeople and hippies, blue-collar workers and homeless side by side, and together they studied the Bible. He demonstrated through his actions that we are "all one in Christ Jesus" (Galatians 3:28). As his MS progressed, he had good days and bad days. He was honest and transparent about this. He experienced major depression and would ask me how to forgive abuse and trauma. I would share with him my own revelations and breakthroughs. On the good days, he discipled me, and on the bad days, I discipled him.[6] Heroes exist on both ends of the rope, and sometimes they swap leads.

Being a disciplemaker is a little like being the leader on an instructor-training trip. You are there to help people learn to be guides themselves. While they should be able to do a lot of things on their own and take care of themselves, they still need advice, direction, and a place where it is safe to be unsure of themselves. As a good guide trainer, we listen with respect, looking to give them the little nugget of wisdom they are missing. We also listen with an ear to what God might say to us through them and look for what we can learn from their experiences.

No hero is meant to pursue the journey alone. We all need friends, allies, and fellow sojourners to share with us and shape us. As a discipleship guide, you get to connect the disciple to a community of believers and help them build life-changing relationships. The powerful simplicity of transformative relationships lays the foundation for challenges ahead.

Discussion Questions

1. How can we learn to hear the voice of God through the people we are discipling?

2. How can we address our fears of transparency?

---

[6] Being loved well by this man and his family has been one of the greatest privileges of my life.

3. How can we encourage and cheer on each other as a community of disciplemakers?

4. How can we better connect to one another as disciplemakers to help create a networked community of disciplemaking?

Inventory

At the beginning of the chapter, we looked at this Scripture passage:

> Dear, dear Corinthians, I can't tell you how much I long for you to enter this wide-open, spacious life. We didn't fence you in. The smallness you feel comes from within you. Your lives aren't small, but you're living them in a small way. I'm speaking as plainly as I can and with great affection. Open up your lives. Live openly and expansively!
>
> 2 CORINTHIANS 6:11-13, MSG

How does the Scripture sound to you now? What new meaning does it carry for you?

What revelations or insights are you taking away from this chapter? Capture them here:

Revelation/Insight #1

Revelation/Insight #2

LIVES CHANGED

EXPERIENCES REVELATION

LEARNS NEW THINGS

FEELS THE STRUGGLE

TEAMS WITH OTHERS

ANSWERS THE CALL

ORDINARY PERSON

DISCERNS THE SEASON

5

LEARNS NEW THINGS

The Way We Change

You've all been to the stadium and seen the athletes race. Everyone runs; one wins. Run to win. All good athletes train hard. They do it for a gold medal that tarnishes and fades. You're after one that's gold eternally.

I don't know about you, but I'm running hard for the finish line. I'm giving it everything I've got. No lazy living for me! I'm staying alert and in top condition. I'm not going to get caught napping, telling everyone else all about it and then missing out myself.

1 CORINTHIANS 9:24-27, MSG

IT WAS ABOUT 5:00 A.M. AND THE SKY was starting to turn light. As the sun's rays arced around the curve of the earth, only the red wavelengths of light reached us on the mountainside. The result was a snow glacier awash in soft pink. This brief phenomenon, called alpine glow, lasts only about twenty minutes, and it is one of my favorite things in all of creation.

We had been walking since 2:00 a.m. Starting from the camp, we had trekked across rock and dirt wearing hiking boots until we had reached the snowfield about an hour later. I had brought two sets of snow boots on the expedition, one light pair for warmer weather and one heavy pair. Current conditions were warmer, so I laced up the lighter pair at the edge of the snowfield.

This was my first expedition in three years. To prepare, I had spent many hours in my heavy glacier boots on the stair-climber at the gym, ignoring the curious looks I got from people. After all, feet make or break a climb. But now, as I enjoyed watching the rock and ice increasingly redden with the impending sunrise, I became acutely aware of the blister forming on the outside of my left foot. This was not good. Really not good. I had trained for months for this. Others were depending on me. But I had trained exclusively in my heavy boots and not worked out in these lighter shoes even once. I was about to torpedo the climb because I had failed to properly condition my feet to my boots.

One of the top reasons expeditions fail is because of improper footwear or boots that are not broken in. It happens all the time. In my case, all the training I had done was rendered useless because it did not prepare me for the real-life situation I faced on the mountain. There are effective ways to train and ways that are mostly a waste of time. How do you know which is which? By discerning how relevant and applicable that training is to real life.

Discipleship is the same way. When we take a step of faith to follow Jesus on our journey, we learn to practice what he teaches us. The process of transformation happens through learning and unlearning. Like the way a person's back becomes familiar with the weight of a pack, we become aware of Holy Spirit's prompting through regular practice in the simple moments of normal life.

The marker of good training is that we can put it into practice. As my boots showed me, it is not how you perform in the gym that counts, but how things go on the mountain. That's why in this chapter we're going to explore how to teach and learn in ways that make transformation easier.

Every hero, every disciple and disciplemaker has challenges he or she must face. Each of us needs to remember truth when it really matters—truth like who God really is and who we really are. Helping people learn well, remember well, and transform is the goal of every good guide or mentor.

PERSONAL REFLECTION

What is something you've experienced that you might consider to be training or preparation in your own life? What was that like? How did it transform you?

No Blank-Slate Discipleship

The first thing we need to keep in mind when it comes to training and preparation is that everyone comes to a discipleship conversation with preexisting thoughts, ideas, and experiences. That means, in order to call people to "unlearn," we must first recognize they have originally "learned" something.

One thing I often see in discipleship curriculums or programs is the default assumption that the student has never heard about God and does not know anything about God. But no human being is a blank slate. Each person you meet has lived every day of their life before you came along. And if you believe that God is active in the world, then we can also profess the truth that Holy Spirit has been pursuing them, speaking to them, counseling them, comforting them, and guiding them *every day of their life before they met you*. What a fantastic and freeing promise!

Have you ever had a bad habit that made learning a good habit harder? Most people have the habit of grabbing onto things, like a rope, when they are afraid of falling. But in climbing, that is extremely dangerous. If a person gets scared and grabs the rope instead of the rock, they end up holding their own weight instead of trusting the person whose job it is to catch them if they fall. To climb safely, they need to unlearn what they have learned before.

Many ideas and behaviors exist in a person's life before they are intentionally mentored in them. This is true for a person climbing a wall, and it is true for people when it comes to discipleship. God has been guiding them. They have seen sin, they have heard the whispers of the enemy, and they have heard the whispers of Holy Spirit. As a disciplemaker, you need to respect this. You can't assume what people know and what they don't know. And you can't assume that what they think or believe lines up with Scripture and the character of God. This is precisely why we need discipleship through conversation. We need to know and not assume. We need to know their story, what their experiences are, and what took root in pivotal moments—the truth or a lie.

The disciple's previous experiences and how God has

already been leading them on their Hero's Journey is a treasure for both of you. It reminds you that you are not responsible for God's part of disciplemaking. God has been working with the person before you arrived on the scene and will be working with them after your season as their disciplemaker ends. Explore the foundations God has already laid. Ask Holy Spirit what the goals are and join the work already in process.

Facts or Freedom?

How do we help those we disciple not just know more about but also be changed by the Trinity? First, we need to remember that there is a difference between teaching and discipleship. As we've talked about before, giving Jesus greater lordship of our lives doesn't just happen from simply listening to sermons or reading books.[1] Hearing information is not

Disciplemaker Pro Tip:

To prompt conversations around someone's core beliefs, you can use a discipleship curriculum, a book, a workbook, a sermon series, or the content and challenge that comes from life itself. As you do, explore what is being revealed about God and discuss it. Talk about what you think and why. And remember, a "fact" cannot easily replace a lie. The person will have to *experience* the truth somehow, either through time or through revelation.

---

[1] It takes many, many hours of listening to teaching to create change. This method of learning is slow and quite unreliable. Consider that it is estimated to take ten thousand hours to become an expert in something, but then add in the reality that the normal rate of recall is only about five minutes of forty minutes of content by the next day (if you are taking notes; it is much less if you are not). Let's say that forty minutes is the sermon you listen to in church every week. At that rate, if you faithfully attend one service a week, taking notes and being a good student, it will take 140 years to reach expert level. That's why passive learning is not an effective method for disciplemaking.

enough—it must be followed with obedience. For example, I know that sugar is bad for me, but I drink the soda or eat that cookie anyway.[2] We need to know things in a different way for those truths to change our lives.

When Jesus says, "You will know the truth, and the truth will set you free" (John 8:32), the word he uses for "know" is the same word that is used for knowing someone intimately. So the truth that sets us free can never just be a fact we have memorized. It must be something we know both experientially and emotionally—or, according to Jesus, we don't really know it at all. The good news is that the way God created us to learn is much more amazing and simple, and anyone can do it!

A little science can revolutionize how we think about learning. We have all heard people say things along the lines of "I know it in my head. I just need to know it in my heart." There is something to that. Neurologically speaking, "head knowledge" and "heart knowledge" are two distinct types of long-term memory: *semantic* and *episodic*.[3]

Semantic memory is your collection of data, facts, and concepts, similar to the kind of information that helps you win money on *Jeopardy!*

Episodic memory includes procedural memory, or muscle memory. Procedural memory is how you brush your teeth, how you drive to work, or other motor actions you can do without much thought or attention. Episodic memory also includes your autobiographical memory: the memory of your personal history or your story.

---

[2] Mmmm . . . cookies.

[3] F. I. M. Craik and E. Tulving, "Depth of Processing and Retention of Words in Episodic Memory," *Journal of Experimental Psychology-General* (1975): 268–294.

Not surprisingly, semantic memory, or *Jeopardy!* data, is easily forgotten. If you don't use a memory fact, it gets removed. At one time, you probably memorized the presidents of the United States or the capitals of major countries. How many of those can you recall now? Our old, unused memories are trashed.

Autobiographical memory, however, is a much stronger memory system because it is interconnected with empathy, compassion, and other social emotions, and with our body systems, like heart rate or fear response. Because autobiographical memory is the memory of your story, it is intertwined with your identity as a person. Your brain is *very* invested in keeping autobiographical memories. In fact, when we start to lose them, we call that "dementia," and it terrifies us.

Now for the super interesting part: Remembering your history involves the same brain process that thinks about your future. Autobiographical memory is the *only* memory system that can project into the future or answer the question "How can I apply this to my life?" Semantic memory cannot do that.

For example, try to apply a semantic memory—like "Who was the first president of the United States?"—to your future. You can't because it is a fact and is stored in the wrong memory system. The fact that George Washington was the first president of the United States has no bearing on your life tomorrow.[4]

Here is the kicker: If we teach in a sermon that "God is good," our brain receives that as a data fact and stores it in

---

[4] This is true unless, of course, George Washington did directly affect your story or the story of your people. Then it is part of your collective memory, and you can think about what it means for your life.

semantic memory. But what happens when we expect a person to apply that data to their life? The biological reality is that they *can't*. It has been stored in the wrong memory system. When we teach biblical or spiritual facts and then expect people to walk them out in their lives, we are asking them to do something that is not biologically possible. To apply a biblical truth to their life, a person must learn it in their autobiographical memory.

Discipleship is incredibly difficult, if not a biological impossibility, when our only method is teaching to the fact memory system through lecture. Expecting head knowledge to become heart knowledge is not how God created us to learn.

However, if we have conversations about life around biblical truths, and we practice living out those things in community, then those truths are much more likely to be stored in our autobiographical memory. I learned in Sunday school that I was supposed to love my neighbor and be kind to others, no matter how they treated me, but this lesson did not hold deep meaning for me until I had a really mean neighbor whom I had to choose to serve anyway.

When we see someone offering forgiveness instead of seeking revenge; when we see someone choosing to trust God as they nurse a sick child; or when we see someone sharing their home with the poor, we see them walking their Hero's Journey as a disciple. This helps us understand what it means to live out the truths of Jesus. When we apply how God created us to learn disciplemaking, the truths about God can *easily* become part of a person's story—quickly remembered and automatically integrated into their lives.

PERSONAL REFLECTION

Think about something that you know that you know. How did you learn that? How much was data learning a part of it? How much was experience a part of it?

Training for Transformation

A good guide trains someone so they are not only competent and safe when they are together, but also safe when the guide is *not* present. As disciplemakers, we want someone to live the life of a disciple when we are there to belay them. But it is vital for them to know how to climb—to journey—without us as well. We want them to learn in such a way that they become a guide and make disciples themselves.

Each of us can be more effective at the Great Commission if we partner with God's brilliance and work with how he made people to learn and grow. With a few different simple approaches, we can follow God's leading and help the truth of the gospel and the Kingdom be more real to people—so it becomes part of their story, the fabric of who they are and how they live.

Parables

Have you heard the parable about the two climbers who descend from a long day only to run into a large bear at the bottom of the cliff? They both take off running only to find out the truth: You don't have to outrun the bear, you just have to outrun your partner.

Parables are a great method of simply illustrating deep concepts. Jesus taught with parables, and like parables in the outdoor adventure world, some were meant to make people uncomfortable. Parables activate and connect with the autobiographical learning systems because people can imagine themselves in those same circumstances. When you use a parable, you're not spouting a theory disconnected from life but describing a tangible metaphor that illustrates a deeper truth.[5] Jesus used parables to connect spiritual truths to the everyday circumstances and experiences of regular life, teaching the mysteries of the Kingdom in ways that people could touch, taste, hear, smell, and feel.

Like Jesus, we can use stories and illustrations to help make abstract concepts real for people. Going deep into the meanings of the Greek and Hebrew words or the cultural nuances of Scripture are not the best methods of transformation for most people. Now, don't get me wrong, we need to read and understand the Bible! But we also need to use illustrations that people can relate to intuitively, like modern parables.

Testimony

Sometimes Jesus helped people come to greater understanding by sharing part of his own story (e.g., Luke 4:16-23; John 5:16-45; John 6:35-40). Personal stories and testimonies are another means of connecting to autobiographical memory. When I hear your story, I remember my own. I compare my story to yours. I think about how they are similar and how they are different. I consider how I would feel in your circumstances

---

[5] When we teach disconnected concepts, we lose the power to communicate truth and instead just puff ourselves up with knowledge (1 Corinthians 8:1).

and whether I would respond in the same way. This process activates empathy in the brain and builds compassion.[6] We can't help but imagine ourselves in the shoes of other people.

As a disciplemaker, tell your stories. You can talk about how God taught you things or made Scripture come alive to you. Talk about the painful lessons and the revelations that cost you. Share the truths God has worked deeply into your soul and how that happened. Your testimony is *very* powerful (Revelation 12:11).

In the biblical sense, while a story is an illustration, a testimony is a *revelation*. The testimony of a person's relationship with God carries within it the power of heaven to transform lives. Any person can minister to any other person when they are sharing out of their testimony. No matter what you don't know about God or the Bible, you know *some little nugget of revelation* about who God is and what he has done. Your testimony can change someone's life.

Immersion

Immersion is a powerful disciplemaking technique. Jesus modeled this with his disciples; they went where he went and did what he did. First, the disciples watched Jesus heal the sick and cast out demons (Matthew 4:23-25; Mark 1:21-34; Luke 4:38-41). Then he sent them out two by two to do the same thing (Matthew 10; Mark 6:7-13; Luke 9:1-6). Jesus was constantly giving his disciples opportunities to try things out, to learn from experience (from success and failure), and then he would debrief afterward.

---

6 Remember mirroring from chapter 4—that is the foundation for empathy.

For example, in Luke 10:17-24, the disciples were amazed that the demons submitted to the name of Jesus. Jesus affirmed that was true and the authority he had given them was even greater than that. But then Jesus also reminded the disciples that both of those truths were small in comparison to a greater truth—their names were written in heaven and they were seeing what centuries of prophets had wanted to see. In debriefing their experience, Jesus helped the disciples better understand what had happened. Then he put it in the larger context, building the bigger lesson.

As a disciplemaker, we can help others continue to build lesson upon lesson. We can help them reflect upon their revelations. We can show them connections in Scripture so that they can discover the treasures contained in the Word of God. We can help them see things in a bigger context. The lessons of experience are not fodder for sermonizing, but for helping those we disciple discover, reflect on, and refine their unfolding story as a follower of Jesus.

Immersion experiences can exist right where you are. They can occur when a group engages in a task or activity and then discusses it afterward to unpack what God was showing each person. Missions trips, outreach, business done with a Jesus-Kingdom heart, living life as an active disciplemaker, and serving in ministries of the church can act as immersion experiences, but *only if* they are accompanied by intentional reflection and debriefing.

Programming and Teachable Moments

The wilderness ministry I worked for provided immersion discipleship experiences where small groups would camp, hike, backpack, rock climb, and snow mountaineer. We traveled from camp location to camp location, carrying everything on our backs. We lived together, struggled together, overcame together, and worshiped together. We did this as an intensive experience designed specifically to teach character and build our identities in Christ. As leaders of the ministry, we needed to know who people were, journey with them, pour into them, and prepare them to lead quality trips without us.

During one season, some of the wilderness instructors did not feel up to the task of telling the stories or teaching the same way the key leaders did, so I tried a rhythm of highly scripted, highly programmed discipleship conversations. Instead of feeling better equipped and supported, the instructors ended up feeling frustrated, fettered, and unable to meet the needs of the students as they surfaced. Prescribed words did not equip them for all the divine appointments.

In another season I tried the opposite—a rhythm of being completely nonprogrammed and fully Spirit-led. It was also a complete failure. The lack of structure left the leaders lost, and the quality of the trip experiences were all over the place. Students commented that it often felt "preachy." We learned that it was inappropriate to leave the instructors entirely on their own.

Neither tactic created the disciplemaking results we wanted. So we learned to balance the right amount of structure with the right amount of Spirit-led conversations. We changed the program so that key intentional conversations happened on key days, which allowed flexibility for the open-handed conversations needed to address what was happening in the group as it arose. We found the sweet spot, giving instructors the structure they needed to keep the students' journeys moving forward and the freedom to meet the needs of the moment.

You may know how to walk a disciple through a curriculum or set of devotionals, but it is just as important to know how to leverage a teachable moment. Here's how you can turn an experience into a teachable moment:

1. Discern the teachable moment (notice that *something* happened and pause).
2. Discern the internal process (character to be formed): *What is God doing to bring greater wholeness, and how can the disciple participate in that?*
3. Discern the external process (obedience to be lived out): *What is the response that will help them live toward obedience to God?*
4. Ask why and a follow-up question.
5. Repeat.

Afterward, when debriefing the whole experience, here are some questions you can ask:

1. What just happened? (What did God do? What did others do? What did you do?)
2. When has God done something like this before? (In Scripture or in your own life?)
3. What does that tell you about God?
4. What does this tell you about yourself?
5. How can you live in alignment with that truth?

I have a friend who is really good at this. She loves to hear what is happening in other people's lives. She asks great questions like "What is God showing you these days? Where did you recently experience wonder? Or what is a breakthrough you are contending for in your life or the life of another?"

As an observer of people, she watches and then asks great follow-up questions, like "What did you mean when you said . . . ?" or "What was going on in your heart when you did . . . ?" She listens to their responses and discerns from Holy Spirit if there is a teachable moment to step into *and* if the time is right to unpack it.

Apprenticeship

When a person decides to walk alongside another in relationship and learn from them in their everyday life, this is called *apprenticeship*, and it's a powerful form of intentional discipleship. In apprenticeship, the lessons and questions are set in the moment, and everyday life is the curriculum.

Regularly, people who attended our wilderness programs would choose to stay, work for the ministry, and be apprenticed—and these apprenticeship relationships lasted about three years. Some were shorter and some were longer, but we found that it took a little more than a year of doing life together to really get to know a person. About twelve to eighteen months in we would usually hit the point of deep transformation. This often looked like a series of hard conversations where the disciple would be faced with what God wanted to do in their heart and life. They would get to choose to go through the hard thing and find breakthrough—or choose not to. Many submitted to the discipleship process, and the community around them supported and encouraged them. It usually took about another twelve to eighteen months for the adjustments to take hold and the breakthrough to be completed.

Cynthia was a professional in her late twenties when she found SROM on a random internet search. She began to cry as she read the page about the deep discipleship experiences. Within a couple of months, she quit her job and moved from Texas to Wyoming, unsure of what God was doing but confident he was up to something.

About sixteen months in, Cynthia was struggling. She was angry and frustrated, feeling pressed on all sides. As God increased the pressure, Cynthia cried out to him. We had been watching Cynthia and knew a serious conversation needed to be had, but God had not yet released anyone to do it. We sensed he wanted to press a little longer. The intensity increased for about another month—and then God said it was time. I don't know what happened between Cynthia and God, but God opened the door for a deep conversation with her.

Cynthia was firmly but gently confronted about her selfishness and transactional way of living and being in community. This was hard news to hear, and it broke her heart. In that moment, Cynthia could have called it quits. She could have packed her bag and walked away, but instead, she allowed herself to be sweetly broken. She spent an entire day crying and facing the truth of herself. She spent the next day having one-on-one conversations with her coworkers and housemates, repenting of her behavior, her attitude, and her selfish heart. She promised to do things differently.

It was dark and painful, but step-by-step Cynthia made a

drastic metamorphosis. She went from helping others only when it was convenient and she got something out of it, to being one of the most servant-hearted people I know today. When her season at the ministry ended, she went back to school and started a new profession helping the sick and infirm. Cynthia bravely submitted to the discipleship of the community, and the entire course of her life changed.

+ + +

Experiential learning, revelation, and testimony allow for learning to be life changing, as opposed to simply learning facts that we can either agree or disagree with. I am of the strong conviction that propositional truth[7] is a weak discipleship method and that it literally educates us beyond our obedience.[8] Jesus' life, on the other hand, demonstrated that we can *experience* the truth, *feel* the truth, and *know* the truth. If something doesn't change our lives, then we have not learned it the way Jesus intends.

If we're going to live out a truth, it needs to be something that *we know that we know that we know.* When we come to a moment in a real-life challenge or struggle, we need to know what our truths are and who God really is. Like a person who knows how to stop a fall on snow with an ice axe, we

---

[7] Propositional truth, in philosophy as well as much of Christian apologetics, is the idea that a person can be convinced of the "truth" through proposing an idea and then debating the evidence for or against it. The individual judges the evidence and renders a verdict of "true" or "untrue." Since it is a purely semantic memory exercise (so it can't be walked out), it reduces faith to intellectual assent, and sets up people as the judge of truth. There is nothing biblical about it regarding either truth or discipleship.

[8] Dallas Willard is historically credited with stating that many Christians are "educated beyond their obedience."

need to be able to respond the right way when it matters. If a truth doesn't become embedded in our autobiographical memory, other beliefs or experiences will shape our thoughts. We all hold beliefs that contradict the truth of Scripture, and we need to uncover and untangle those beliefs so that they can be addressed and replaced with something stronger that sets us free. When we do, we can live a life that demonstrates the light of truth and dispels the darkness—and we can live like Jesus would have if he walked our hero-path.

PERSONAL REFLECTION

What are five key truths you know that you know that you know? What is an example of each truth from your life that you can use as a testimony to share with someone else?

Discussion Questions

1. Recall the two types of long-term memory. What are two or three implications of each for how we can help others learn new things?

2. Think about a transforming life lesson from the last six months.

   • Which of the methods described in this chapter (parable, testimony, immersion, apprenticeship, or teachable moment) did it include?

- How did the learning happen?

- What about that lesson should you share with someone else?

Inventory

At the beginning of the chapter, we looked at this Scripture passage:

> You've all been to the stadium and seen the athletes race. Everyone runs; one wins. Run to win. All good athletes train hard. They do it for a gold medal that tarnishes and fades. You're after one that's gold eternally.
>
> I don't know about you, but I'm running hard for the finish line. I'm giving it everything I've got. No lazy living for me! I'm staying alert and in top condition. I'm not going to get caught napping, telling everyone else all about it and then missing out myself.
>
> 1 CORINTHIANS 9:24-27, MSG

How does the Scripture sound to you now? What new meaning does it carry for you?

What revelations or insights are you taking away from this chapter? Capture them here:

Revelation/Insight #1

Revelation/Insight #2

LIVES CHANGED

EXPERIENCES REVELATION

LEARNS NEW THINGS

FEELS THE STRUGGLE

TEAMS WITH OTHERS

ANSWERS THE CALL

ORDINARY PERSON

DISCERNS THE SEASON

6

FEELS THE STRUGGLE

Listening to the Right Voices

We put no obstacle in anyone's way, so that no fault may be found with our ministry, but as servants of God we commend ourselves in every way: by great endurance, in afflictions, hardships, calamities, beatings, imprisonments, riots, labors, sleepless nights, hunger; by purity, knowledge, patience, kindness, the Holy Spirit, genuine love; by truthful speech, and the power of God; with the weapons of righteousness for the right hand and for the left.

2 CORINTHIANS 6:3-7, ESV

WHEN I FIRST BEGAN TO ADVENTURE OUTDOORS, I did not know how important it was to listen. Children, after all, tend to just blaze forward, a little awkward and overconfident. To help me understand why I needed to listen, my dad told me about one of the first people to die on a guided trip on Denali. Some new expedition guides with a different company had ignored my dad's advice about how to set up a snow camp, which involved probing for crevasses and marking out the edge of the camp's safe area with flags. But the leader of the expedition took several short steps outside the probed area, fell into a two-hundred-foot hidden crevasse and was killed instantly. Maybe the guide of the expedition was not paying attention. Maybe he had not taken my dad's consulting seriously and thought a few extra steps were no big deal. Either way, there was only a body to recover.

The story got my attention then, but when I became responsible for training other guides, the story terrified me. Ignoring advice because of pride or suspicion, or because you think you know more, can have a devastating impact. I knew I had to be humble enough to listen to the wisdom God provides through various avenues—and I had to figure out how to teach others the humility to listen, learn, and be wise when stretched beyond their expertise. There is nothing so sobering as being in over your head.

Listening in the Unknown

I'm infamous for a few decisions at the wilderness ministry: taking the instructor staff winter camping in -30 degrees F for five days; doing snow travel training in a blizzard; requiring new instructor staff to identify native trees while camping during a tornado. (In my defense, I didn't know it was a tornado. Wyoming is normally really windy, and I didn't want the new staff to think they could hide in their tents when the weather was less than ideal.)

Each of these decisions were not accidents—they were intentional choices. I wanted to stretch the instructors so they could learn they were capable of more while they were still in the safety net of our guidance as senior leaders. I wanted to learn who they were in threatening moments so that I could speak life to them and disciple them then and there. I wanted their hardest challenges to be ones they faced with us, so that they would keep their head and not abdicate their role when they were without us. If I challenged them myself, I hoped they would not be overwhelmed when they faced an emergency or significant situation.

The commitment of the community, combined with the effective teaching and learning techniques, created a space where they could grow and increase their capacity as leaders and as disciplemakers. They learned how to stay present when things got really hard (tests). They discovered what they were good at (strengths). They saw and faced the unredeemed parts of their heart or character (inner weaknesses). And they learned to press into God and hear what Holy Spirit was saying in the middle of everything.

Sometimes when life gets harder and we face trials or increased challenges, we want to retreat and hide or be defensive and fight. But this is not what Jesus calls us to do. Jesus asks us to do something much harder: reach out and hold on to one another. As a disciplemaker, your presence helps the disciple do what they could not do on their own.

So far we have talked about being intentional in both relationships (teaming with others) and training (learning new things), but how do we follow Jesus deeper into the unknown so we are truly changed? Creating security as we move further into the unknown requires two things: learning to be led by the Spirit of God and learning our own voice.

Listening to Holy Spirit

Not too long ago I wanted to go surfing for my birthday. I have useful core skills—excellent balance and white-water rafting experience—but I still needed someone to help me. I needed a guide. When we move into new places, we always do better when we're with someone who already knows the terrain. And in disciplemaking, no one knows more and is a better guide than Holy Spirit.

We've been exploring how to learn in a way that transforms us and brings freedom, but there's a reality we need to reckon with: Our brain ignores about 99 percent of the information it takes in.[1] Additionally, the human brain modifies and filters most things we see or read (and it makes up a ton of stuff[2]), all without asking our permission. So, though we like to think we are reasonable and objective, we cannot trust our brains to be accurate.

Because God made us, he's very aware of this. In fact, God did this on purpose. He created us so that we can't know the truth on our own—we need help. Jesus told his disciples, "But when he, the Spirit of truth, comes, he will guide you into all

---

[1] Tom Valeo, "Where in the Brain Is Intelligence?" Dana Foundation (website), April 4, 2008, online article, Dana Foundation, https:Dana.org.

[2] Super nerd moment: Your left temporal lobe is dedicated to keeping a coherent narrative of events, and it will make up reasons for things that best fit the rest of your worldview. For example, I could do an experiment on you and use tricks to make you behave in a certain way. Then if I asked you about why you behaved that way, your left temporal lobe would make up a reason that has nothing to do with me, since you were unaware that I was influencing you. The reason may be plausible, but it would be inaccurate. For more, see Antonio Damasio, *Descartes' Error: Emotion, Reason, and the Human Brain* (New York: Grosset/Putnam, 1994).

the truth. He will not speak on his own; he will speak only what he hears" (John 16:13, NIV). We need Holy Spirit to lead us into all truth because our minds cannot find it by themselves. We need to be Spirit-led.

Holy Spirit is our greatest ally and can help us know what to say and do as we disciple others. And as we follow the lead of Holy Spirit, we must teach the person we disciple to do so as well. One proud moment for me as a disciplemaker was when a member of our neighborhood faith group exclaimed in the middle of a debate, "Just because you are a pastor doesn't mean you are the only one who hears God. Maybe God can speak through us too!" She won her point.

Holy Spirit's leadership in disciplemaking is essential because, as we've talked about, each person is an individual, not a formula. We need to make disciples *specifically* and not generally. When you fit a pack, you adjust all the straps to fit the person's body. If you fail to do that, the pack rubs wrong and can create injury. The same is true for how we use the Bible. Scripture gives us the general principles of how we are to live as God's people, but only the Spirit-led, specific application of the Word can help us encourage and challenge an individual.

Being Spirit-led is an essential aspect of what it means to live as a disciple of Jesus and his Kingdom. Just like I needed to teach my instructor staff to be safe without me, we need to teach those we disciple to be able to hear Holy Spirit for themselves as well. And if we are going to reproduce disciples who are dependent on Holy Spirit, then those we are discipling must first see us depending on Holy Spirit for wisdom and revelation.

Disciplemaker Pro Tip:
We need to allow Holy Spirit to lead the disciplemaking process or we end up relying on ourselves and our own understanding. When we begin to think we need to know all the answers, we can feel inadequate when we realize we don't know everything, or we can take it personally and feel rejected when someone we are discipling disagrees with us.

Listening to the Spirit's leading is our most unused faith muscle. We must learn to exercise it. Unfortunately, how to listen to Holy Spirit might be one of the most debated things in Christendom. I think this is because God is personal and speaks to each of us individually in a way we can hear. While that makes us feel special, it also makes the experience of hearing God's voice hard to validate (scientifically speaking). Hearing God is much more art and heart than science and mind.

Hearing God is like recognizing a song from the first few musical notes. The more we are in the Bible learning what God says, the easier it will be to recognize his voice among all the others in our head.

Here are five simple principles and three simple ways to practice hearing the voice of Holy Spirit:[3]

Principles

1. Anything you hear and/or sense should line up with Scripture.
2. Don't be too directive (no names or dates, for example, "You're going to marry Taylor on April 23").

---

[3] For some great practical resources on this, check out: https://accessibleprophecy .com/2018/06/22/revelation-a-heart-to-know/ and https://accessibleprophecy .com/2018/05/16/revelation-ears-to-hear/.

3. Everyone hears God uniquely. It could be words, feelings, pictures, colors, songs, or any other creative way God made you to hear him.
4. Spirit-inspired "messages" or "words" for others should always be given with a caveat that you could be wrong.
5. Any conviction should be life-giving, moving you toward God and not further away. It should bring hope and increase faith and never bring shame or fear.

Practices
1. Write down what you hear, sense, or feel from God. Pray over it for a day or more. Notice if what you're hearing resonates with your heart and gets stronger or if it lessens as you take it to him.
2. Bounce what you think you are sensing off the person who is discipling you.
3. If you believe in an angry God, you will hear an angry God. Keep pursuing intimacy with the love of God so you hear his voice clearly.

God is always speaking, singing, loving, painting, dancing, and abiding with you. The closer you are to him, the more you will be able to discern what he is doing and saying.

If you are a disciplemaker, eventually someone will come to you and say, "I heard God say . . ." Just as it is important to learn how to hear God's voice, it is also important to learn how to test a "word" from God. There are many voices in our heads—ours, our family, our influences, God's, and our enemies. How can you know the difference? Since there is some degree of uniqueness in how we each hear God, discerning voices can feel tricky. This is why we need each other and a faith community. Testing a "word" is a *group* assignment. No "word" is pure and unaffected by our humanness. Your community can help you let go of what you *think* you hear and trust God to prove what is from him.

Here are some of the questions to ask within the context of community:

1. Does it line up with Scriptures[4] God has the person focusing on?
2. Does it harmonize with Holy Spirit's leading around the topic? Does the Spirit-led sense in others confirm it? Does it resonate with those who are investing in the person?
3. Is it something the person would say to themselves, or is it totally different? Is there someone else whose voice it is most like (a parent, a mentor, their own)?
4. What is God showing through reality that confirms the truth of the word? Things God says will eventually come to pass. Things made up by our minds or others will not.

There are a few ways I discern whether something is from God. First, if the "word" is not something I would say to myself—if it doesn't sound like me at all—that's a big sign that it might be God's voice. Second, I know to pay attention when the word resonates somewhere deep inside of me and

---

[4] Many people use Scriptures out of context, including the enemy. That is why it is not enough that a Bible verse was used. Holy Spirit needs to affirm that the Scripture being used is the right one at that time.

immediately brings a fruit of the Spirit (faith, hope, love, joy, peace, and self-control, among others)—that's a sign God is in it. Third, sometimes it is easier for me to recognize the enemy's voice than tease apart and distinguish the other voices. If I recognize the enemy's voice in the "word," I remember he is a liar. I may not know what to do, but I know I should do the opposite of whatever the enemy tried to talk me into.[5]

Remember, God is optimistic about the future and will bring life even in the midst of struggle. If what you hear brings discouragement, depression, or fear, you might be listening to the wrong voice.

When you are seeking Holy Spirit's direction for a choice, how do you know what to do? How do you sort through the possibilities, instincts, advice, and concerns?

Here's a helpful pathway:

- Identify what choice is the fear-based option and what choice is the faith-filled option.
- Once you identify the faith-filled option, talk to God about your fears.
- Write down the promises he gives so that you can reread as needed.
- Ask God what happens if you screw it up and get it wrong.
- Write down his affirmation in that space too.

Learning to hear God is like identifying birdcalls. Each bird has its own song. Some birds have a morning song, a night

---

[5] These days I also continually lay my decisions and thoughts before the Lord. I ask him to derail or resist me where I am wrong, not just bless me where I am right. My heart is open to his direction. This helps me move forward in the confidence that if he wants me to know something, he can get my attention.

song, a mating song, and a grieving song. Teaching someone to hear the different songs of God equips them not only to be a hero but to guide others on the Hero's Journey as well.

PERSONAL REFLECTION

Describe a time when you knew Holy Spirit was speaking to you. What are some ways you connect with feeling Holy Spirit move? What are some ways you connect with hearing Holy Spirit speak?

Listening to Yourself

My husband, Bob, took a swift-water rescue training with five of his kayaking friends. They were boating down difficult rivers together and wanted to take the course to all be on the same page. Over three days, they learned both skills and more about each other. They learned that Jeff could *not* throw a rope, but he could expertly navigate his boat to any point on the river. Bob was slower at knots than Lucas, but he could see the whole situation and what needed to be done in an emergency. They learned that no one was good at everything. Everyone had strengths, and everyone had limitations. As they embraced who they each were, and what they were each good at, they were empowered and celebrated for what they *specifically* had to bring to the table.

God knows who we are and how he made us, with our own personality and strengths and weaknesses, and he has called *us* to make disciples. God asks us to make disciples without asking us to change our specific mix of personality and spiritual gifts. People connect with God in different ways, and they respond naturally to different personality types. So all kinds of disciplemakers are needed.

Disciplemaking is not done by factory-line workers who build Jesus-like widgets, doing the exact same thing in the exact same way. It is done by the breadth of humanity, seeking to reach the breadth of humanity! Ephesians 2:10 says that we each are God's *poema*—God's specific work of art. We are all part of an epic poem, each of us writing a line in the middle of our ordinary days. As the person we disciple lives their life, they are writing the lines of their poem, and we get to help them hear what God wants to author.

As we learn, listen to, and understand our unique designs— and the designs of those we disciple—we gain insight into the different ways people can be used by God. Our hand-crafted humanness can often be overlooked when it comes to disciplemaking, but it is vital to how we disciple others.

Introverts and Extroverts

Think for a moment about a person you would consider to be a disciplemaker. Reflect on their behavior and social interactions. Would you say they are more of an introvert or an extrovert?

The people we think of as disciplemakers are often extroverts. They fill a room or have no problem speaking to groups of people. They are naturally outgoing, and people are drawn to them. But it would be a mistake to confuse being extroverted with being a good disciplemaker. Remember, disciplemaking requires listening to Holy Spirit and coming alongside another person as a helper and mentor. Simply being social or speaking to a group is not the same thing.

This confusion has created several faulty lines of thinking. The first is that introverts may not see themselves as qualified to make disciples because of their shyness or lack of comfort in social situations. The second is that extroverts may mistake preaching and large-group interaction for successful discipleship, neglecting the deep work of relationships that disciplemaking requires. Disciplemaking needs all of us and all our unique personalities. Introverts and extroverts both need to consider how their personalities can lend themselves to making disciples.

When introverts embrace their God-design, their quiet influence carries wisdom and stability. Introverts naturally have patience for others and take the time to listen to Holy Spirit, considering things in light of what God is saying. They create space for depth and reflective processing.

Our disciplemaking programs often don't do a great job making room for introverts, which is why introverted disciplemakers are invaluable. If you're an introvert, you can connect with those who are also introverted and show extroverts how to care well for them.[6] Disciplemaking for you may look less like conversation in person and look more like written dialogue or texting. You or an introvert you're discipling may not be comfortable sharing thoughts in groups larger than three or four. Introverts do better either in one-on-one settings or listening to others talk while focusing on a task (like grilling, dishwashing, or helping in some way). As you disciple, remember that introverts

---

[6] As a more extroverted person married to an extreme introvert, I took a year and experimented with trying to experience things, like church, as an introvert. It was eye-opening. Some churches, like those that were liturgical, were nice. Others, like the evangelical and Pentecostal churches, were simply exhausting for me. If you don't understand why, ask an introvert.

are exceptionally good at paying attention and picking up on things without necessarily having to interact with anyone. Allow time and space for those observations to surface.

Extroverts, on the other hand, can find relationships easy to start and are comfortable in groups of people. Small groups are good places for extroverts to externally process with others. In fact, external processors really need the space to talk and discuss in order to know their own thoughts and feelings. That's why having a disciplemaker to help them unpack things is important. Extroverts often need more than one disciplemaker in their life at a time.

When discipling an extrovert, give them the space to talk things through and work it out in conversations. If you are an extrovert, remember as a disciplemaker that you need to give space to others to think and process. Slow down and be patient. Don't try to fill spaces of silence—let them linger. Leave space for Holy Spirit's voice. Use your natural relational ease to pursue people and draw them out, but remember to let people express themselves in their own way. Let your energy create a safe space for people to learn, grow, and share (or not).

APEST: Superpowers for Normal People

Almost everyone has a favorite superhero, usually because of the superpower that makes them unique. Disciplemaking is the same. People have diverse personalities, which means they disciple others in different ways. That diversity mostly centers around a person's personality and capacities according to Ephesians 4:11.[7]

---

[7] Ephesians 4:11: "Now these are the gifts Christ gave to the church: the apostles, the prophets, the evangelists, and the pastors [shepherds] and teachers" (NLT).

If you want an in-depth look at the five ministry gifts of Jesus, check out my book with Alan Hirsch, *Activating 5Q: A Users Guide*. But in brief, Jesus has gifted the following capacities to the church:

> A—apostolic: entrepreneurial, innovation, architecting, strategist, explorer, pioneer
> P—prophetic: truth-telling, passionate, artistic, reforming, justice-seeking, God-seeking
> E—evangelistic: mobilizing, recruiting, promoting, connecting, motivating
> S—shepherding: caring, protecting, reconciling, peace-making, nurturing
> T—teaching: organizing, investigating, accuracy-seeking, wise, curious, legacy-building

To be clear on our assumptions, these capacities are not offices, titles, or other forms of power. Rather, they are a mindset and a lens through which we see the world (like compassion, justice, and truth). We are each more passionate about some, and less passionate about others. But the ones that are our primary strengths significantly affect how we think about and approach discipleship.[8] Each of the five gifts of Jesus emphasizes a different *priority* in disciplemaking.

- *apostolic*: focuses on making discipleship scalable and reproducible; emphasizes discipling someone as they disciple someone else

---

[8] Go to https://5qcentral.com/tests/ to take an assessment. Your primary gift tends to be the lens in which you see the world. Your secondary tends to be the voice in which you speak.

- *prophetic*: focuses on hearing Holy Spirit in disciple-making; brings challenge to help a person be who God created them to be
- *evangelistic*: focuses on living as a visual aid that demonstrates the Good News of Christ in disciple-making; encourages following the example set by the life, person, and practices of Jesus
- *shepherding*: focuses on having a healthy community life in disciplemaking; elevates living in reconciled relationship with others as brothers and sisters
- *teaching*: focuses on understanding the Bible in disciple-making; cares about having effective ways of learning

Just because one of these is a leading priority based on someone's gifting and makeup doesn't mean the others aren't vital for a holistic approach to disciplemaking. Can we disciple well . . .

- without learning about God's message to us in Scripture? (T)
- without asking God for his insight on the situation as made known through Holy Spirit? (P)
- apart from being in community? (S)
- without our consistent reorientation to the person and example of Jesus? (E)
- without setting the expectation from the beginning that they are also meant to make disciples? (A)

The answer to each of these is, of course, no. Working with whatever content, curriculum, or method you may use in discipleship conversations, you need to always seek to include the following:

- connecting it to the Kingdom of God (A)
- bringing in the voice of God (P)
- bringing in experience (E)
- bringing in the community (S)
- bringing in Scripture (T)

What does this look like practically? Let's imagine Jerome was grumpy about someone else at work getting a promotion instead of him. He was wondering if it was a sign that he needed to find a different job. His disciplemaker decided to discuss five APEST-oriented questions with him to help him process the situation:

A: What are you called to do? Are you called to be in this job? Are you called to something else?

P: What is God saying to you right now about this situation?

E: How can you walk this out in a way that looks like Jesus to those around you?

S: What does your family/community feel about the situation? How is it impacting you as a spouse/parent/friend? What does loving others well look like?

T: What is God challenging you with right now in Scripture? What passage reminds you of your situation? What is a passage that describes what God wants to give you in this circumstance?

Each of the five gifts of Jesus is needed to make healthy, holistic disciples. But no single person is really good at all five. God in his brilliance created us with limitations and inherent weaknesses—and he called it good! Just as my husband and his friends needed each other's gifts to be holistically safe on the river, we need each of these gifts in community to make healthy disciples.

PERSONAL REFLECTION

Are you an introvert or extrovert? How do you think that affects the way you personally disciple others?

What is your APEST profile,[9] and how do you think that impacts how you think about discipleship?

Counterfeit Voices

In the outdoor world, whether you're mountain climbing or white-water rafting, you'd be wise to avoid joining teams with people who are in it for themselves. Though they may have strong talents and skills, they are not an asset to the team. People who go it alone, who aren't interested in the team, get themselves or others hurt. Likewise, we need to be disciplemakers who are not in it for ourselves or who make it about us.

There are voices in our lives that give us bad counsel and pull us away from the wise path. That's why not knowing who

---

9 See https://5Qcentral.com.

we are or not accepting our limitations can create issues. We get distracted trying to be someone we are not, making it hard to hear Holy Spirit through the noise of our unaccepted soul. The more you know your own authentic, God-given voice, the better you can distinguish it from the voice of Holy Spirit, and from voices of treacherous imposters. They are counterfeits of the voice of God's wisdom. These voices give you bad advice and lead you into danger.

The Voice of Narcissism

A narcissistic disciplemaker thinks the relationship is about them. The root of this can vary, but they may feel this way because they're trying to prove their role in the church or their calling from God; they may falsely see the disciple as a feather in their cap; or they may be motivated by a desire to show off their knowledge to others.

The Voice of Perfectionism

Sometimes a disciplemaker can mistake another's journey as a direct reflection of their own, buying into the lie that they must be a perfect guide or mentor. Their identity is wrapped up in the success or failure of those whom they disciple. The perfectionist disciplemaker views asking God for help, as well as any pain or struggle in the relationship, as a sign of failure.

The Voice of Power

The power-driven disciplemaker has a vision, a calling, or a passion, and recruits other people to *their* cause. For them, disciplemaking is more about having a "follower" than about serving God. This person sometimes mistakenly calls people *their* disciples when only Jesus can call disciples to himself.

Scripture says that no one should be called the disciples of Paul or Apollos (1 Corinthians 3:3-7). We are disciples of Jesus and his Kingdom. A disciple never belongs to an individual—they only belong to Jesus.

The Voice of Performance

A performance-driven disciplemaker holds a belief or expectation that everything should just "be better" because Jesus is in the picture.[10] They can lack patience with the process of growth, change, and formation. Yet God seems content with change taking days, years, even generations. He holds time in his hands and seems confident in his ability to manage it. The quick-fix mentality will not help us get anywhere fast but will only make us frustrated.

The Voice of Individualism

Individualism can be an asset for pioneering new places or ideas, but it is not an advantage in discipleship. We have many reasons that we want to be on our own: efficiency, woundedness, communication struggles. But we are called to be a collective—to be the body of Christ. Don't be an independent eyeball[11]—be part of the body.

---

[10] One time, my husband was having a bad day and, in a moment of desperation, I told him to just clap himself happy. Like Tinkerbelle. We were very newly married, and I have grown significantly in my patience and compassion since then. But we still use "clapping yourself happy" as a joke to remind ourselves it is okay to have a bad day.

[11] No zombies for Jesus, please.

+ + +

The journey of discipleship refines not only the disciple but also the disciplemaker, helping expose the wrong voices you may be listening to and acting out of. As you go deeper into the unknown with those you disciple, submit any of your own sinful issues to God and allow him to bring greater wholeness.

Here are some additional red flags to watch out for as a disciplemaker:

- Piling strict rules or heavy burdens on the disciple, instead of helping them learn things slowly and deeply
- Undermining the disciples' familial or covenantal relationships
- Isolating the disciple from the teachings, influence, or leadership of others
- Allowing the disciple to idolize the disciplemaker
- Expecting blind obedience or unilateral submission
- Forcing transparency and trust to be out of pace with one another
- Hanging on when it is time to let go

We are each susceptible to at least one of these counterfeit voices or red flags, which is why it's important that we are connected and accountable to our own disciplemaker. If you see something coming to the surface that is not Christlike, make sure you dialogue with your own disciplemaker. We are all a work in progress and on our own Hero's Journey as a disciple. Life shapes us as a disciple and helps us be a healthier disciplemaker.

PERSONAL REFLECTION

Which counterfeit voice is the most tempting for you to listen to? Why? Take a moment to ask Holy Spirit to help keep you from being drawn in by that voice.

Going Beyond

As the hero journeys further into the unknown, change gets harder and more significant. This is because, as we are on a journey to the heart of God, he is also on a journey to go deeper into our heart. We equip the disciple for that journey as we help them learn to trust others, lean into transformational learning, and build relationship with Holy Spirit as he prepares them for deep work—work they could never do without a guide.

As the journey changes us, we come to realize how consumerism and individualism work together to talk us out of the superweapon of discipleship—which is dying to ourselves. If we are a disciple of Jesus, we are called to pick up our cross and follow him. If we are a disciplemaker, we are called to lay down our life for the sake of the Cross and the Kingdom. But many times, we just don't want to die to ourselves. During the struggle, we'll feel tempted to turn around. But the journey so far has prepared us and sets us up for success in the transformation of our heart. We can feel the struggle, and we can endure.

Discussion Questions

1. What experiences do you have collectively in listening to Holy Spirit? What practices do you have as a community

to help discern what God is saying or to "test a word" so that you can be clearer and more confident about it?

2. How can we help each other be healthy disciplemakers?

3. How can we support and empower others to become healthy disciplemakers?

Inventory

At the beginning of the chapter, we looked at this Scripture passage:

> We put no obstacle in anyone's way, so that no fault may be found with our ministry, but as servants of God we commend ourselves in every way: by great endurance, in afflictions, hardships, calamities, beatings, imprisonments, riots, labors, sleepless nights, hunger; by purity, knowledge, patience, kindness, the Holy Spirit, genuine love; by truthful speech, and the power of God; with the weapons of righteousness for the right hand and for the left.
>
> 2 CORINTHIANS 6:3-7, ESV

How does the Scripture sound to you now? What new meaning does it carry for you?

What revelations or insights are you taking away from this chapter? Capture them here:

Revelation/Insight #1

Revelation/Insight #2

LIVES CHANGED

EXPERIENCES REVELATION

LEARNS NEW THINGS

FEELS THE STRUGGLE

TEAMS WITH OTHERS

ANSWERS THE CALL

ORDINARY PERSON

DISCERNS THE SEASON

7

EXPERIENCES REVELATION

Becoming Motivated by Love

Are you tired? Worn out? Burned out on religion? Come to me. Get away with me and you'll recover your life. I'll show you how to take a real rest. Walk with me and work with me—watch how I do it. Learn the unforced rhythms of grace. I won't lay anything heavy or ill-fitting on you. Keep company with me and you'll learn to live freely and lightly.

MATTHEW 11:28-30, MSG

NERVOUS FACES REFLECTED THE FIRELIGHT. Keeping company with their own emotions, the team stared quietly at the campfire flames. Every so often, the wood would pop and release sparks and smoke into the crisp night air. Brooding looks were broken only by sips from a water bottle or cup of hot cocoa. Tomorrow was going to be a big day—the peak attempt. A 2:00 a.m. wake-up, roped snow travel across the glacier in the dark, roped snow climb until they reached the summit or 1:00 p.m., whichever came first. Nervousness was appropriate.

Yasmin was the first to speak up about her fears. Doubt and worry had been simmering in her heart and mind all day. Her voice wavered as she bravely named what she was feeling. As a recovering addict, she said she was familiar with letting people down. Now, on the eve of the climb, she was afraid the pattern would repeat and her rope team would fail because of her.

Her instructors encouraged her to pray, but that idea only brought up bigger, deeper fears. She had not done enough good to deserve God answering her prayers, she said. So many times in the past she had prayed and God seemed to ignore her—and she knew it was because she was an addict and God was punishing her because of her sin.

Yasmin's instructors sat with her, heartbroken. "God is not that way," they encouraged her. "You don't have to earn his approval through good works or worry about his rejection when you screw up." Yasmin heard that they believed it, but she did not. Anxiety shook her body, bursting out of her in short, sputtering sobs. The mountain ahead mirrored the mountain of failure in her heart.

We have come far on our journey together learning about God's desire for all believers to make disciples. Looking back over our path so far, we heeded the call to embrace discipleship as a Hero's Journey of becoming more like Jesus. Fortunately, we can do this together in community, coming alongside one another as hero makers and guides. As we journeyed further, we learned about how to facilitate transformation and how to listen to Holy Spirit. We have also discovered how our story contains treasures and revelations that God gave us to help others with their own journeys.

But where exactly are we going on this journey? What has

all the learning been preparing us for? As a disciplemaker, what am I helping someone "overcome"?

In my twenty years of teaching people how to be disciplemakers, the greatest challenges I have ever encountered are not the devil, sickness, injustice, or demonic strongholds. As great as these are, the external struggle is never as great as the internal one. Our most imposing mountain, the biggest adversary that we face in this life, is the motivation within our hearts. Facing our wrong motivations and unearthing the ones that compel us to live into the abundant life are the most important parts of us to be remade.

False Summits

I was about twelve years old the summer my grandmother woke me up early for a long hike in the Tetons. Coffee had not yet been introduced into my life, so all I could do was follow behind my grandmother on the trail as my brain slowly warmed to the day. For the first little bit, the trail moved easily through the trees. But two miles in, the path turned sharply upward, and we started to quickly gain in elevation. Rocky switchbacks took us up the steep mountain face and above the trees.

I remember looking around as we climbed and noticing what mountain peaks were to the left and right of us. Given our location, we had to be hiking up the Grand Teton! It was a mountain I had wanted to hike, and I was thrilled that we were going to the climber's camp just below the cliff faces. For miles I paced my steps with my breath and enjoyed the views of the Snake River Valley.

The switchbacks got shorter and shorter, and around mile

six, we turned a corner of trees and rocks to discover a small, beautiful, alpine lake. The cold water was so clear, I could see all the way to the bottom. "I didn't know there was a lake on the side of Grand Teton!" I exclaimed to my grandma.

"We are not on the side of the Grand," she said. Confused, I looked around more carefully. The Grand Teton loomed large overhead. I could see a rock spire jutting up from behind the lake, but behind that was a lot of space. A giant chasm lay between the mountain I was on and the one where I wanted to be. I walked around, looking at the rocks from different angles and trying to make sense of the optical illusion in front of me. We were not on the side of the Grand Teton. We were on something different, disconnected from the mountain where I thought we were.

"This is called Disappointment Peak," my grandma said. It was a prophetic statement: Disappointment was exactly what I was experiencing in that moment. My heart fell. The lake was amazing and all, but all that effort and I was only climbing a false summit.

False summits are one of a climber's greatest frustrations. They feel like the summit but are not, in fact, the top. And sometimes they are completely disconnected from the actual summit—a huge cliff or gap makes reaching the summit impossible. They are at best a distraction and at worst a trip killer.

As a disciplemaker, I have learned that our profound, internal struggles tend to emerge from one of two significant counterfeit versions of discipleship.

False Summit #1: Being a disciple of Jesus is about behaving the right way.

Many times we are lured into the belief that discipleship is defined by our behaviors, such as Bible reading, praying, tithing, obeying the Ten Commandments, and so on. But any one of us can behave appropriately and still live a life that does not bring God glory. The Pharisees "behaved" according to the rules and followed them strictly, but their hearts were far from God (Matthew 15:8). God isn't looking for a set of behaviors. *God is looking for a heart that is transformed by his love.*

All the major religions of the world have the same basic list of expected good behaviors: pray, be still, be kind, read the holy texts. Simply being good is not the substance of Christian discipleship. For the Christian disciple, all the challenges must lead us to a deeper experience of the lordship of Jesus and his Kingdom—to the transformation of our hearts. As disciple-makers, we must keep this in mind and not get distracted by "behavior." If we disciple in the realm of right behavior, then we will accidentally teach people to be performance-oriented toward God, unintentionally causing them to feel they have failed or are rejected when they don't behave appropriately. Neither of those perspectives is healthy for a disciple. Shame, guilt, and fear are not what God has for us. We must help those we disciple begin and continue their journey in freedom.

False Summit #2: Being a disciple of Jesus is about learning the right information

In this counterfeit, discipleship looks like a long checklist. And that's a problem because *how* we present the content of discipleship is what people will believe *is* the process of discipleship. If we make discipleship about reading or listening to sermons, then people will think following Jesus is merely about information.

But we can't reduce the amazing adventure of discipleship to a classroom curriculum or a book to read (including this one).

That's like looking at a picture of a mountain instead of being on the side of one. Life with God is so much more amazing and awe-inspiring than how much information a person can remember.

Discipleship needs to be about the heart, first and foremost. If we focus on the heart, the heart can teach the mind.[1] As we explored in chapter 5, if a person learns something in their autobiographical memory and it is part of their story, then they can learn to articulate it and teach it to others as revelation. Out of the heart comes our behavior, our words, and our desires for our community.

✛　✛　✛

These discipleship "false summits" give us a sense of accomplishment. But they distract us from the real challenge we are meant to overcome. And when we notice, name, and are able to ignore the two distractions of behavior and information, we can focus on the real work of disciplemaking—discerning motivation.

What's Your Motivation?

In Luke 15:11-32, Jesus told a parable about someone who chose rules and behavior over relationship. Often referred to as the story of the Prodigal Son, the story is really about *two* sons, both of whom have lessons to teach us. And while we tend to focus on the younger brother and his journey, the older brother's story is much more disturbing.

At the beginning of the story, the younger brother prematurely asks for his inheritance, essentially telling his father

---

[1] Be aware of texts that are merely self-help or about how to live your best life now. They are more likely to disciple you on the "kingdom of me" than the Kingdom of God.

that he wishes his father were dead. He wants to move on with his life without his father. The older brother also receives his inheritance but does not leave. Instead, as the older child, he stays on the family land, which was most of his inheritance.

Usually, we think about the younger son's rebellion and the shame it brought to his family, but the older brother also dishonors his father. Rather than rebelling through his behavior, the older brother rebels with his heart.

The father is available to show love to his eldest son and teach him everything he knows. But instead of learning from his father and living as a son, the older brother is working and toiling in the field. He doesn't reject his father by running away like the younger brother; he stays and rejects the father to his face. Something is very broken in the older son's understanding of the father. In essence, the older brother is living as a slave, trying for some reason to earn what is already his.[2]

When the older son sees the party held in celebration of his brother's homecoming, he begins to complain. The father, as gracious and patient with the older brother as he is with the younger, endures the shame of leaving the party and goes out to speak with his son. It is in this short exchange that we see the warped motivation of the older brother. "All these years I've been slaving for you," he says, his words dripping with venom and barely concealed rage towards his father. He continues with his accusations, telling his father that he has never given him "even a young goat so I could celebrate with my friends" (Luke 15:29, NLT). But the truth is, that the house, the animals, and the servants all belong to the older brother. He

---

[2] See Galatians 4:1.

could have had a party at any time. The older brother could have celebrated life at any moment in the house of his father. Instead he distanced himself from his father, trying to earn his father's love through obedience—trying to gain an inheritance that was already his. His main sin was turning his relationship with his father into something transactional.

The hardest part of the parable is its tragic ending, with the older brother standing outside the house. We never know what he chooses. The younger brother "comes to his senses" and returns home. But does the older brother ever let go of his broken understanding of who the father is and go *into* the house?

PERSONAL REFLECTION

Which of the two sons do you identify with and why? In what ways have you made your relationship with God transactional?

This parable shows us vividly how our relationship with God can be based on one of two things: *rules* or *love*. In both types of relationships we can behave in a proper and righteous way. The "doing" part of each relational motivation looks the same. They both have the same *practice* of doing good.

From the outside, it can be hard to tell what type of relationship a person has with God—a *law-based* or a *love-based* relationship. We cannot discern motivation simply by observing exterior behaviors or actions. Instead, we need to look a little closer and ask a few questions, which is why disciplemaking is all about asking the follow-up question.

Rules

In a law-based or rules-based relationship, a person does "good" to gain a reward or avoid a consequence. Their good actions are motivated by either earning something good or avoiding something bad. For example, someone with a law-based mentality would choose not to speed out of fear they might get a speeding offense.

As a disciple, this can manifest in a variety of ways. The "doing good" might be going to church, reading the Bible, praying, or tithing. But our motivation is about what we are trying to gain or avoid. We can be reading our Bible or going to church to gain God's approval. Our tithing may be motivated by a belief that people who don't will suffer financially. Or we might pray because we want the outcome of God doing what we ask.

For many of us, law-based motivation is the way we were

taught to interact with God. When I was younger, I was taught to do good things so that God wouldn't be disappointed with me. This may be your story too. Perhaps, like me, you gave your life to Jesus to avoid a consequence, such as hell or death. Or maybe you gave your life to Jesus to earn something, such as a place in heaven or the approval of someone important to you.

But here's the truth: If you do the good thing as an attempt to gain blessing, favor, or approval, those things will not come. You can do the right thing for the wrong reason, and it can become death to your soul.

Think about the Pharisees. They had hundreds and hundreds of laws they were supposed to follow, and they kept creating more. They, like the rest of us, preferred the structure and stability of laws. *Law* is easier because it draws lines of who is in and who is out. But Jesus often confronted the Pharisees that though they behaved according to the laws they were taught, they falsely believed in the strength of their own righteousness to save them—and they missed the heart of God and his mission (Matthew 23).

Having a law-based relationship with God was destructive for the Pharisees and the communities around them. It is destructive to us and our communities of faith as well.

PERSONAL REFLECTION

Think about your life as a disciple. List some things you want to gain or avoid and what you are doing to gain or avoid that.

Love

In a love-based relationship, we do good things without thinking about the consequences. At the beginning of our chapter, Yasmin was afraid to rope up because she wanted to avoid letting her team down. But the team promised to love her whether they reached the summit or not. Instead of being motivated by the outcome or consequences, God wants us to be motivated by our affection for others. When we are motivated by love, we don't think about what we want to gain or avoid. When we care for someone, we do the good thing because we are motivated by how we care about the other person, not because there is something in it for us. In fact, sometimes it costs us and is not always beneficial. But we do the good thing because that is what love does. What comes next does not change what we choose to do.

Why do you call or send someone a note for their birthday? Are you trying to gain favor with them or avoid a negative consequence? Or is it because you care for them and want to show them your love on their birthday? Only love is a motivation strong enough for us to endure on a dangerous journey potentially full of trials and heartache. Only love motivation brings life (1 John 3:14).

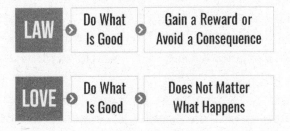

PERSONAL REFLECTION

What is one good thing you do simply because you love someone, without thinking about the consequences?

Did Jesus come to earth to save us because he was trying to gain or avoid a personal consequence? Or did he come to earth because he so loved us and desired to be close to us, that he died for us with no guarantee we would ever love him back? Jesus chose us and continues choosing us, regardless of whether we will choose him back. That is love motivation. God does not make us love him back, but he does what is good anyway.

As a disciple, we should do good things, such as pray, read the Bible, gather with our brothers and sisters, tithe, and care for others—not out of a legalistic expectation of behavior, but out of a response for what God has done for us. We forgive because we have been forgiven. We talk to God because he has given everything to talk to us. We are faithful to read the Bible because God has been faithful throughout human history to write down the things he wants us to know about him. We pray for the sick and go to those who are oppressed because Jesus left the glory above to make the Kingdom tangible in our midst, and we want everyone around us to experience the goodness of life in the Kingdom too. Because we see the good that Jesus did and are thankful for it, we do the same.

Being with God, says pastor and disciplemaker hero Debbie Mares, is not a discipline—it is a pursuit based on desire. And so our role as disciplemakers is not to tie people up to law-bound behaviors (Galatians 3:1-5). Instead, we are to help them discover the depths of God's love and a life of responding to his voice. This is the deep work of redeeming the heart, where increasing freedom and security with God creates an overflow we share with other people.

PERSONAL REFLECTION

What is one example of a good thing you do because you love God and just can't help yourself?

+ + +

Motivation is everything. In the parable of the two sons, the younger brother was love motivated, returning home because he knew his father was kind and would feed him, even as a servant. But the older brother's transactional heart was motivated by law. If earning accolades or avoiding consequences is why you do something as a Christian, I have some tough news for you: The Bible says it won't work.

> If God's promise is only for those who obey the law, then faith is not necessary and the promise is pointless. For the law always brings punishment on those who try to obey it.
> ROMANS 4:14-15, NLT

At one time I lived without understanding the law. But when I learned the command not to covet, for instance, the power of sin came to life, and I died. So I discovered that the law's commands, which were supposed to bring life, brought spiritual death instead.

ROMANS 7:9-10, NLT

He has enabled us to be ministers of his new covenant. This is a covenant not of written laws, but of the Spirit. The old written covenant ends in death; but under the new covenant, the Spirit gives life. The old way, with laws etched in stone, led to death, though it began with such glory that the people of Israel could not bear to look at Moses' face.

2 CORINTHIANS 3:6-7, NLT

Here is the hard truth: Good works motivated by love yield good fruit, but good works motivated by law bring death. You can live a transactional, law-based life with God, and it will bring destruction. Or you can do the good thing because of love, and life will come to you and those around you.

We need to live in the truth that God wants us to have a real relationship with him and not be focused on simply trying to avoid his wrath. God is not cruel, and when we act as if he is, then we demonstrate that we don't know him at all. God leads us from a place of love, not punishment. He wants us to do good because he has gone first and made a way for us to love. He wants us to serve him because we know we are loved and are set free.

A Child of the Father

The enemy would love nothing more than for us to believe that God is distant, disappointed, or holding out on us. He wants us to think we must perform or be righteous for God to love us. This is so he can point out our flaws and cause us to feel shame, rejection, and unworthiness.

Each Hero's Journey has its temptations and trials. There are good days, rainy days, days where you take the wrong trail, days when the stove breaks and you eat cold soup. But here's the truth: Things that steal our joy are inner battles around our identity as a child of God.

Our position as a child of God is current and real (Colossians 1:13). He doesn't give us a narrow mark to hit but a large field to play in. He cares about life, freedom, and delight, not perfection.

Moreover, God loves all his children equally. In fact, God loves you as much as he loves Jesus (John 17:23, 26). At Jesus' baptism, *before* he did one day of ministry, *before* he passed the temptations of the wilderness, and *before* he laid down his own will and chose the cross—before any of that—God spoke over him and said, "You are my dearly loved Son, and you bring me great joy" (Luke 3:22, NLT). Jesus had not *done* anything, and yet the Father was pleased with him. *The same is true for us.* Do you know that you know that you know you are a beloved child of God? Do you know that he is well pleased with you right now?

God is a good parent. He does not withhold love or affection from us if we get into trouble or don't try our hardest. We don't have to perform to get close to him. In fact, he wants us to be like a little child (Matthew 18:3-4). Little children are needy, impulsive, make all kinds of messes, get it wrong, and have no clue about a lot of things. Like the rest of us, they need to be encouraged, treated kindly, and loved well.

This is one of the reasons God sent Jesus—to model how a child of God lives, acts, loves others, and receives love from a lavish God.[3] It is also why God asked us to *disciple* one another and not just *teach* one another. We need guides to show us how to do things and help us when we struggle. We need relationships, and we need someone to love us when we get it wrong. As a disciplemaker, you get to model the heart of God to the person you disciple.

As disciplemakers, we stand with God's other children against the lies of the enemy that say we must earn God's love. When we talk to the person we are discipling, we can help them discern *why* they are doing something. Are they doing a good thing because it is what Jesus is asking them to do? Or because they are trying to gain a predetermined outcome? Are they doing good out of a response to the love of God and seeking to love him back? Or are they following a set of rules someone handed to them?

---

[3] Jack Frost, *Experiencing Father's Embrace* (Shippensburg: Destiny Image, 2006), 59, 77.

God's love is there, always and unconditionally. This is the revelation that changes everything for us and for those we disciple. The mountain of law motivation crumbles. Shame, guilt, and fear are powerless before this love.

Realizing our identity as a child of God is the core focus of discipleship. When we embrace the journey of a hero and hero maker, we realize that all other things flow out of this. We get to choose the kind of son or daughter we will be. It is up to us how we live this life, what we do with this gift, and what we pass along to others. And when we fully embrace the all-consuming, seemingly reckless love of God, when we step fully into our identity as sons and daughters of the King of the universe—then we are unstoppable.

One Step at a Time

The process of discerning identity and motivation and guiding a disciple toward revelation may feel daunting. But remember, every mountain is climbed one step at a time. Looking at the whole thing can be overwhelming. But every mountain can be broken down into sections, and sections can be broken down into steps. The same is true when it comes to the transformation and redemption of our hearts. As a disciplemaker, part of your responsibility is to hold the disciple accountable for their response to whatever God is teaching and revealing to them.

Accountability can be a confusing term. Most of the time we associate it with punishment, mistakenly believing that accountability involves the ability to apply a consequence. But accountability is merely the *ability* to ask people for an

Disciplemaker Pro Tip:
When you are holding a disciple accountable to deep change, their efforts to be different will almost always fail at first. That is predictable and okay. Challenging or encouraging the disciple toward different behavior is exactly where you must start. But it is highly likely that the disciple will hear the change to be love motivated as a "rule" to be followed. It will take time and revelation for that motivation to come from a deeper place.

account of their actions. All that is required is a good relationship and the permission to ask the disciple, "Why?" or "How are you doing with . . . ?" It is that easy.

Doesn't accountability cause people to act out of law motivation? you might wonder. At first, yes. But as the disciple finds that they are unable to follow through with the action/behavior in their own strength, that initial failure opens up an opportunity to go deeper. You can begin to ask the disciple questions to uncover what belief or thought underlies how they are behaving (not how they want to behave). As the person explains what they are doing or thinking, you respond with, "Okay, but why?" Affirm what the person is saying but keep going deeper. You need to be patient and let them wrestle to find the next answer, only helping if they are really stuck. Keep repeating the question until they get down to the bones of their motivation and belief system.

My husband, Bob, works in Information Technology (IT). At one point, he served as the entire IT department for a medium-size business. He was good at his job, but he was also a little, well, grumpy. People started avoiding him and stopped asking him for help. His boss, Steve, who was a Christian mentor to us, called Bob into his office for a chat. He pointed out Bob's attitude toward everyone and how they were responding. He talked about the stereotype of the grumpy IT guy and asked Bob point-blank, "Is that the kind of person you want to be?"

That question forced Bob down to the bones of his behavior. Yes, he wanted to be better than that. But as he searched his heart and talked to God, he realized he was mad at God for taking away the stable academic job he'd previously had. Bob needed to forgive God for the job change and repent for judging God about it. When he stopped being mad, he started to see himself as someone who could help others in the office with the things they could not do for themselves. His whole internal attitude and external posture toward his job changed.

When you're willing to go deeper with your questions, you can help the disciple identify what lies or unbelief they are holding on to. Then you can use God's Word to help replace them with truth. You will know they have grasped the truth when they move forward successfully in the act of obedience, because now it will be motivated by love and not law.

There are five steps of transformation that you can walk the disciple through:

1. Becoming aware of the issue
2. Committing to change a behavior or thought pattern
3. After initial failure (almost always happens), identifying the underlying commitment or belief that undermines the "good" thing to do

4. Repenting for the motivation, belief, or idea that God is doing it wrong, and confessing the lordship of Jesus over their head, heart, and hands.

5. Asking God for one new thought of truth and one new habit of love to move forward in

No matter what, regardless of the fear, doubt, or anger the disciple may feel, encourage them to never stop dialoguing with God about what they are going through. It is okay for them to ask God, "What the heck are you doing?"[4] The Psalms are a great place to go whenever they need help articulating their mixed feelings toward God.

+ + +

Your role as a disciplemaker is to help the disciple consider who God is calling them to *be* before thinking about what God is calling them to *do*. When we focus first on what we are supposed to do instead of our relationship with God, we can fall into the trap of being rules and law motivated, which creates an atmosphere of religion. Religion, in this sense, *is where we practice the things of Scripture, where we do the "good," but we are not connected at a deep level to the author of Scripture.*[5] Paul warned the Galatians of this very trap of

---

[4] Language and tone may vary.

[5] As we disciple someone, we can ask Jesus what he thinks about a specific situation and what specific actions the disciple should take. Advice is good, but it is highly limited, and we want the disciple to grow beyond anything we might say so they can hear from the Lord themselves. Encourage the disciple not to read the Bible simply as a book of wisdom, because it can feel like the advice from one verse contradicts with another. But if you teach the disciple to read the Bible as a letter written directly to them, then Holy Spirit can point out a specific verse or word of wisdom in the moment they need it.

religion: "So Christ has truly set us free. Now make sure that you stay free, and don't get tied up again in slavery to the law" (Galatians 5:1, NLT).

Love motivation creates the freedom to be our true selves, with all our God-given strengths and weaknesses. We have the privilege of helping the disciple on their dangerous journey to discover who God intended them to be, whether they're having a good day or a bad day. Because their relationship is no longer about performance, they are free to seek more about God and what it means to be his child. Then out of love they will learn to do the good thing. Then a desire to know the God of love will compel them to read the Bible. Then their worship of him will be an overflow response, rather than a duty. And in the spacious grace of being God's child, we will see the Kingdom come on earth as it is in heaven.

Discussion Questions

1. If you came to Jesus out of a love motivation, consider sharing your story. How can we help people move from being law motivated to being love motivated?

2. If we want to be more love motivated, what is something we need to start? Stop? Adjust?

3. How can you help the people you disciple discern between sin, spiritual warfare, God's refining fire, and the fallen nature of life?[6]

Inventory

At the beginning of the chapter, we looked at this Scripture passage:

> Are you tired? Worn out? Burned out on religion? Come to me. Get away with me and you'll recover your life. I'll show you how to take a real rest. Walk with me and work with me—watch how I do it. Learn the unforced rhythms of grace. I won't lay anything heavy or ill-fitting on you. Keep company with me and you'll learn to live freely and lightly.
>
> MATTHEW 11:28-30, MSG

How does the Scripture sound to you now? What new meaning does it carry for you?

---

[6] Answers will vary based on a person's theological background.

What revelations or insights are you taking away from this chapter? Capture them here:

Revelation/Insight #1

Revelation/Insight #2

LIVES CHANGED

EXPERIENCES REVELATION

LEARNS NEW THINGS

FEELS THE STRUGGLE

TEAMS WITH OTHERS

ANSWERS THE CALL

ORDINARY PERSON

DISCERNS THE SEASON

8

LIVES CHANGED

Experiencing the Kingdom of God

*When I think of all this, I fall to my knees and pray to the
Father, the Creator of everything in heaven and on earth.
I pray that from his glorious, unlimited resources he will
empower you with inner strength through his Spirit. Then
Christ will make his home in your hearts as you trust in him.
Your roots will grow down into God's love and keep you
strong. And may you have the power to understand, as all
God's people should, how wide, how long, how high, and
how deep his love is. May you experience the love of Christ,
though it is too great to understand fully. Then you will be
made complete with all the fullness of life and power that
comes from God.*

*Now all glory to God, who is able, through his mighty
power at work within us, to accomplish infinitely more than
we might ask or think. Glory to him in the church and in
Christ Jesus through all generations forever and ever!
Amen.*

EPHESIANS 3:14-21, NLT

THE CAR SPUTTERED AND LURCHED as Phil angled it over to the side of the road. As it coasted to a stop, Phil's wife, Janie, pulled out her phone to look up a towing company in the area. They were only a few miles outside of town, so hopefully it wouldn't be too expensive. Phil looked at Janie. He knew she would be upset to miss their niece's dance recital this afternoon, but their niece was five and he was sure there would be more opportunities.

Phil looked at the dashboard of the car while Janie gave the towing company their location. He knew the car's mileage was pretty high, but he had no idea what was happening to it now.

"Fifteen minutes," Janie said, as she got off the phone.

Silent tension filled the car while Phil and Janie poked at their phones. Fortunately, Janie didn't ask him any questions. He didn't have any answers.

Twenty minutes later the tow truck pulled over and parked in front of them and the driver got out. He was well over six feet tall and wore heavy, black pants with big combat boots. On his face, he sported a massive red curly beard that left Phil rubbing his jaw in insecurity. Under the rolled-up sleeves of the collared shirt monogrammed with the tow company logo, both arms were heavily tattooed.

Janie scrunched her face in unconscious worry. "I'll talk to him," Phil said as he opened the door and got out. As he walked toward the tow truck driver, he girded himself, unsure of how to play this out.

"Hey-yo! Sorry about your car!" the driver said, flashing a warm smile and holding out his hand to greet Phil. The greeting was so friendly that it took Phil aback.

"Yeah," Phil started awkwardly. "It just sorta stopped."

Phil reached out to shake the man's hand, which was strong but not overpowering. *Adam* was embroidered over the top of the left front pocket of the man's company shirt. "You Adam?" Phil asked.

"Yep!" Adam chirped as he got to work. "I'll get you hooked up right away. You know where you want me to take this?"

"We don't really have a mechanic, so I'm not sure," Phil responded.

"I know the people in town really well. I'd recommend Jim over on Main Street. Legacy Mechanics. But you look him up and see what you think while I take care of this."

Phil walked over to Janie as she got out of the car and told her Adam's suggestion. She spent a few minutes on her phone and then made a call. A minute later Janie told him, "He'll look at the car for no charge and see if he can figure out what's wrong. No cost to us unless they can do something." Well, at least that was some good news.

While Phil and Janie rode in the back seat of the tow truck, he had a chance to study Adam's elaborate and colorful tattoos a little more carefully. On Adam's right arm, Phil noticed a scene of three crosses on a hill with angels hanging over them.

"What do your tattoos mean?" Phil blurted out before he thought about what he was saying. Adam smiled a little bit.

"It's the picture version of the best story I know. I run the towing business for a living. I'm a pastor on the side."

Phil blinked. He had never met any pastors who looked like Adam. Was he the pastor of some sort of cult?

"What's the name of your church?" Janie asked from beside him.

"We don't really have a church building. There are several groups of us who meet in houses once a month for a worship gathering. Otherwise, we meet in small groups weekly for conversation. It's more of a discipleship community than a traditional church. Many of us own and run businesses in town. So it's a kind of a network of people who help each other and live for Jesus," Adam said.

"So you're the pastor . . . you're in charge?" Phil asked.

"Sort of," Adam replied. "We have ten groups of about ten to fifteen people each who meet in people's houses. But each group has its own leader. I oversee the leaders of those groups and the business owners who are part of our network. We see the businesses as ministries to the community. People need affordable services that are run with honesty and integrity, especially when there is an emergency situation, like needing a tow truck."

"That's not like any church I've ever heard of," Janie said, saying openly what Phil was thinking.

"Yeah, I get that a lot," Adam said. "We want to be a group of people who love Jesus and want to live out the things he talked about. The church thing just comes out of that." Adam pulled into the parking lot of the Legacy Mechanic shop. "Jim's a good guy, but if you have any issues, you let me know."

"Is he part of your network of businesses?" Phil asked.

"No, but the coffee shop across the street is. I grew up with Jim; I dated his sister for a while, but that was in high school. Let's just say I know where he lives! But I think he'll do right by you. You let me know either way." Adam reached back and handed Phil a business card with the phone number on it, along with a coupon for two free cups of coffee at the shop across the street.

As Adam processed Janie's credit card on his phone card reader to settle the tow fee, Jim came and introduced himself. Jim said he would need about forty-five minutes to look over the car, so Phil and Janie decided they would wait at the coffee shop.

Efficiently, Adam unhooked the car and drove off, waving to Phil as he pulled out. Phil had not been to church since he was a kid, and Adam was definitely not like any of the pastors he knew growing up. But as the tow truck drove down the street, Phil decided he liked the idea of hanging out with someone like Adam.

Life in the Kingdom

Not too long ago I was visiting Drew's widow, Mary Arnold. I sat in her living room in the morning, reading my daily Scripture meditation, when someone walked in the front door with a ceramic coffee mug. They walked into the kitchen and made themselves an espresso, saying hello to me as they went on their way. I just smiled and shook my head. It was so typical of the family culture the Arnolds had created.

How is a culture like this possible? The person who came in was not one of Mary's best friends. So how, without Mary being present, did the person know they had permission to walk in the front door and help themselves?

This was possible because:

Mary lives an authentic life of discipleship.
She teaches others how to live that same life as a
   disciplemaker.

She helped cultivate a community where many people have that type of authentic relationship with each other.

It is a Kingdom culture where doors are open, permission abounds, and everyone is family. And in this family context, I learned what living and loving like Jesus can look like.

Merely being a disciple is not the goal of life Jesus died for us to live. Discipleship is a vehicle, a method, a journey. But where are we going? We may know what Jesus saves us *from*, but what does he save us *for*? When he asks us to pick up our cross and follow him, where is he leading us?

We get a clue when we look at where we've been and where we're going on the Hero's Journey:

1. We live our Hero's Journey as an authentic disciple under the kingship of Jesus.
2. We mentor someone else through authentic relationship, helping them submit their life to King Jesus on their Hero's Journey.
3. We live changed in this life together, becoming part of authentic community so that we experience the Kingdom and grow in our understanding of it.

Did you know that Jesus taught on the Kingdom of God more than any other single topic? It was his almost singular focus with his disciples. Instead of teaching more rules and law, he painted the picture of the Kingdom with visceral illustrations and vivid colors.

There is a quote I love, commonly attributed to Antoine de Saint-Exupéry: "If you want to build a ship, don't drum up the men to gather wood, divide the work, and give orders. Instead, teach them to yearn for the vast and endless sea."[1] This is what Jesus did with the Kingdom of God.

These days, though, either the Kingdom of God is not taught often, or it is taught as a kingdom of societal and cultural domination that we should be forcing on the world. That is not how Jesus talked about it.[2]

Scripture talks about the Kingdom being both now and not yet; it is already here, and it is still coming. But not because God is holding out on us. He wants us to experience the fullness of the Kingdom now, otherwise Jesus would not have prayed, "Your kingdom come, your will be done, on earth as it is in heaven" (Matthew 6:10, NIV). No, we are the ones who are holding out on God.

We determine how much of the Kingdom we experience, but we're not pursuing it like we should because we hold wrong beliefs. Some people think it is heaven; some think it is church. Many just don't know. But if the Kingdom was important enough to be the thing Jesus taught his disciples about, it should be important to us as disciplemakers also.

The Kingdom and the Church

Asking what the Kingdom is like is the same as asking, "What is the wilderness?" *Kingdom*, like *wilderness*, can refer to more

---

[1] For an in-depth discussion of the quote's origins, see "Teach Them to Yearn for the Vast and Endless Sea," *Quote Investigator*, accessed July 30, 2022, https://quoteinvestigator.com/2015/08/25/sea/.

[2] We are ambassadors of the Kingdom, not colonizers. No one culture defines the Kingdom. Rather, the Kingdom feels the same regardless of the nation or community in which it is found.

than a specific location; it can be more experiential, something we experience in our daily living within the context of relationships. But even that description can't quite capture it either. Maybe that is why Jesus used so many different parables to help his disciples understand the Kingdom.

What we need to understand, though, is that there is an important difference between the Kingdom and the church. These ideas are often used interchangeably, but they are, in fact, two very different things.

Let's refresh our understanding of the two words used throughout the New Testament.

ekklēsia (Greek): a gathering of citizens called out from their homes into some public place; an assembly. *Translated into English as church.*

basileia (Greek): kingship, sovereignty, authority, rule, kingdom, dominion. *Translated into English as kingdom.*

A single follower of Jesus is a disciple, and when disciples gather, they form an *ekklēsia—the church.* But the space where they live and thrive is called the Kingdom of God. The church is not the only expression of the Kingdom any more than one valley is the only expression of the wilderness. The Kingdom of God is no more confined to a building, an event, or a person than it is confined to heaven! The Kingdom can be seen or felt wherever we are—by a lake, at dinner with friends, in our workplaces, as we sit and chat with the homeless. It manifests in quiet and in loud times.

The Kingdom is a mindset we live in—a place of peace,

joy, and freedom. When we are in this mindset, we are living under the rule of Jesus in his Kingdom. When we are not in this mindset, like when we act out or operate in a spirit of control, it's like we left the real life of the Kingdom and plugged into the matrix of the "world" to deal with our situation.

As followers of Jesus, we must learn how to live as citizens of the Kingdom, whether we are gathered with others or not. Jesus taught us to seek first the Kingdom (Matthew 6:33), and so our lives are the journey of exploring the territory or map of the Kingdom, individually and together. That means when we gather as an *ekklesia*, we can celebrate, encourage, repent, discuss, strategize, and send each other out again in hope and faith. The wall between life in the church and life in the world breaks down. We are so ingrained to think in terms of sacred and secular spaces. But bringing the Kingdom into every part of life allows for no such division. We come to understand that God himself is pursuing the world to bring his Kingdom into it.[3] The Kingdom mindset is meant to invade our world, and we can rest in the great grace of joining him in that.

PERSONAL REFLECTION

How have you been discipled outside the walls of the church? How can you disciple outside the walls of the church? If your disciplemaking is currently centered on a church event, what is one step you can take to expand your disciplemaking to a new space or a new time?

---

[3] To be clear, I am not talking about dominionism or theocracy. I am talking about a mindset, a heart disposition. The Kingdom is not about power in any sense that the world wields it. It is about love, freedom, and life.

A greater understanding of how the Kingdom differs from the church helps us begin to see things differently. Life in Christ is not limited to what is happening in our church. Many of us have focused on "doing" the activities of church in the hope that we will make disciples. But Jesus told us to do the opposite. Jesus says if we make disciples, he will build his church (Matthew 16:18). The activities of "church" don't make disciples; disciples make disciples. In the Kingdom we are liberated to bring our life, story, and unique treasures or gifts to the table in *any* environment as tools for disciplemaking.

Jesus Is King of . . .

We cannot talk about the Kingdom in abstract, though, like it is merely a feeling or an idea. A Kingdom, after all, is positional—formed under a King. In the Kingdom of God, we live together under the lordship of Jesus.

Sometimes I think about Pontius Pilate, the lord and governor over Israel in Jesus' day. Because he fought so hard against crucifying Jesus, I wonder if he saw something in Jesus or knew there was something different about him (Luke 23:4). As a Roman, he had a religion and worldview that allowed for gods to walk the earth in human form. But Pilate's allegiance, his vow, was to Caesar. Caesar was his lord, king, and god incarnate. For Pilate, Jesus could be *a* god, but not his personal Lord and King.

We can approach Jesus the same way. Jesus may be someone we respect and admire, and surely a god of some kind, but not necessarily the Lord and King of our daily lives. Yet to be a true follower of Jesus is to see him as both our Savior and King.

Jesus wants more for us than our salvation from death and hell. He wants us to live in the fullness of life in him and others. Our life with Jesus doesn't start when we get to heaven; it starts when we choose to say yes to him on this earth. Giving Jesus full kingship of our life is not something we are able to do in one moment or in one prayer. It is more than a single choice; it requires the reorientation of our whole life. Walking out this transformation in every facet of our lives is what Scripture considers discipleship.

Let's consider what this looks like in a few of those facets:

- Relationships: Think for a moment about your family life, your marriage or singleness, your friendships. Is Jesus king over each of these? God cares a lot about how we behave in our relationships and how we treat one another. It is "part B" of the Greatest Commandment. You can live your life being transactional with the people around you, using them to meet your needs, or you can live with the posture of a servant who knows their worth and loves others well under the direction of Jesus.

  ▸ Are you lord and king over these areas, or is Jesus? How are you living outside the Kingdom here?

  ▸ How can you help a person you are discipling live under the kingship of Jesus and inside the Kingdom in this area?

- Finances: The Bible is full of wisdom on how to manage your money. You can either master it or let it master you. But even that is not good enough for God. He doesn't just want you to be the master of your money—*he* wants to be the Lord of your money and for you to use it under his direction. Jesus wants you to use it for *his* Kingdom, not for your own. Is Jesus king of your money, able to direct you as he pleases? Do you follow Kingdom ways with your finances?

▸ Are you lord and king over these areas, or is Jesus? How are you living outside the Kingdom here?

▸ How can you help a person you are discipling live under the kingship of Jesus and inside the Kingdom in this area?

• Identity: What about your identity, sexuality, and how you see or feel about yourself? The world will tell us many things about our bodies and our sexuality. There are thousands of magazines dedicated to telling us why we are not good enough and what more we can do. But the world is not interested in your heart or your freedom. Only Jesus knew exactly what he had in mind when he dreamt of you. He is the only one who should tell you who you should be.

▸ Are you lord and king over these areas, or is Jesus? How are you living outside the Kingdom here?

▸ How can you help a person you are discipling live under the kingship of Jesus and inside the Kingdom in this area?

• Treatment of Others: The Kingdom rule covers how you treat the opposite sex, how you treat your enemies, and how you act toward authority. God does not abide bullying, taking advantage of other people, power hoarding, or degrading people in any way (1 John 4:20-21). Jesus says we are to treat the most vulnerable the exact same way we would treat him, with honor (Matthew 25:31-46). We are to be kings over no one; Jesus is to be the King of all of us.

> ▸ Are you lord and king over these areas, or is Jesus? How are you living outside the Kingdom here?

> ▸ How can you help a person you are discipling live under the kingship of Jesus and inside the Kingdom in this area?

- **Thoughts and Emotions:** Jesus is not satisfied with one part of you. He wants to be King of how you feel and think. There is no part of our internal thought or emotional life that is outside the boundaries of Jesus' kingship. He cares how you think and feel, even in the deepest parts of your soul.

> ▸ Are you lord and king over these areas, or is Jesus? How are you living outside the Kingdom here?

> ▸ How can you help a person you are discipling live under the kingship of Jesus and inside the Kingdom in this area?

- **Public Witness:** As disciples, our Facebook, Twitter, and Instagram posts, all are subject to the Kingdom rule. They are part of our witness to the world, and the world is watching—closely. Jesus also wants to be King of how you think about the church and your witness on that front. Jesus cares deeply for *all* the members of his family.

> ▸ Are you lord and king over these areas, or is Jesus? How are you living outside the Kingdom here?

> ▸ How can you help a person you are discipling live under the kingship of Jesus and inside the Kingdom in this area?

- Faith Practice: Jesus wants to be King of each and every area of your life, and he is not content to let anything, especially an empty religion, be your king. One of the greatest ways we can find ourselves lost in life is to accept Jesus' wisdom but reject his kingship. If there is anything that upsets Jesus, it is when religion and rules become a substitute for relationship with him (Matthew 15:7-9).

> ▸ How have you let religion be a substitution for a relationship with Jesus?

> ▸ How can you help a person you are discipling connect to the King himself rather than just the "idea" of Jesus?

There is Jesus' Kingdom, and there is a kingdom that is *not* of Jesus. We can either build our own kingdoms and call them businesses, ministries, careers, families, or networks, or we can submit all those things to the rule of the Kingdom of God.

PERSONAL REFLECTION

Where in your worldview have you limited being part of the Kingdom of God that you might need to rethink? What parts of your daily life do you need to be thinking about through the lens of the Kingdom?

We submit to the lordship of Jesus in every part of our lives the exact same way we entered the Kingdom in the first place: repentance. We can't get into the Kingdom initially without it, and any part of our life that is not under the lordship of Jesus only comes under his rule as we repent and submit it to him.

We often think about repentance in terms of our actions and of feeling guilt or shame for past wrongs. But when the New Testament speaks of repentance, the Greek word used is *metanoia*, meaning "change of mind." This kind of repentance is not about regret or guilt or shame. It is about allowing the revelations Jesus gives us through his word, prayer, and relationships with others to change the way we think. Jesus is asking us to turn around, face a new direction, and walk in a different way.

As disciplemakers, we need to help those we disciple to understand and discern how the Kingdom is near in their own lives. Where is God at work? Where are they still acting as king instead of submitting to the kingship of Jesus? Where do they need to repent and believe, move in the opposite direction, and come inside the Kingdom gates?

Repentance demonstrates our recognition of the current reality of our situation. Belief demonstrates our faith in the future promise of

Disciplemaker Pro Tip:
Sometimes you may need to help the disciple take baby steps of faith toward something good when they don't trust it. You may need to help them let go of defensiveness or self-protection and choose to be vulnerable and share their heart. Whether you are guiding them to move away from things that are destructive or toward things that are good, you can disciple someone to seek the Kingdom in all parts of their life.

that reality made whole. "Believing," then, is not just agreeing in our mind but putting our whole life into the hands of Jesus.

As a disciplemaker, you may need to help walk the person through the process of choosing to forgive. Or you may need to help them let go of unhealthy thought patterns about themselves, others, or God. Though it might feel hard the first couple of times, the rhythm of repenting and believing can become life-giving and restorative. Piece by piece, we can move all the parts of our hearts from law to love and bring all parts of our lives inside the Kingdom under the rule of Jesus.

PERSONAL REFLECTION

When was the last time you repented of something? What did God show you he wanted instead? What is an example from your life that you can use to help illustrate the power of repentance for someone you are discipling?

An Ambassador of the Kingdom

The Kingdom of Jesus looks like Jesus. If it doesn't look like Jesus, it is not his Kingdom. And part of looking like Jesus in this Kingdom, Paul tells us in 2 Corinthians 5:19, is to be ministers of reconciliation and ambassadors of the Kingdom.

God does not ask us if we want to be an ambassador for the Kingdom. If we have given our lives to Jesus, we have already been drafted. The question is just how well we live that out.

Your first job as an ambassador is to let the Kingdom be

real inside of you. According to Romans 14:17, the Kingdom starts in you. We must first have a relationship with the King, learning to live and abide in peace, rest, trust, and faith, and having a character like that of Christ. This is a constant and ongoing journey. There is no "arriving" at the place where God has all of you and you have all of God. Not on this side of eternity at least. So we submit ourselves to a life of learning, unlearning, and learning again—the life of discipleship.

Your second job is to bring the Kingdom into your sphere of influence, which includes being an ambassador to others and making disciples. Because you carry the Kingdom and the Spirit of Jesus Christ inside you, you get to bring the Kingdom of God every place you go and change the atmosphere there. This manifests as righteousness, love, peace, joy, and all the fruits of the Holy Spirit (Galatians 5:22-23). Through you, other people get to taste and experience the Kingdom.

Your third job as an ambassador for the Kingdom is to create and live in Kingdom community with others. We can create Christ-shaped community in our neighborhood, our workplace, our friendships, and our family. As we do, we discover that the main purpose of our life is being part of the Kingdom and inviting others into that experience.

PERSONAL REFLECTION

How do you live like an Ambassador for the Kingdom? What is one thing you can teach about Kingdom living to the people you disciple?

Kingdom Community

Imagine a whole group of disciplemaking disciples living authentic lives with Jesus and each other. This is a Kingdom community. As you train others disciplemakers, this is one of the key things to pass down from generation to generation. It is not theoretical or abstract, or something that you must wait until you die to experience. The Kingdom can be real now, in your life, right where you are.

The Kingdom is deliciously infectious. It is the Good News Jesus talked about everywhere (Matthew 4:23). Kingdom community is where people have authentic experiences with God and with others, where they find the Kingdom in the rawness of life and struggle.

We were created to live in and be shaped by community. Being with one another is how we become more like Jesus. Character is not formed in a prayer closet; it is formed in community. This means our experience of the Kingdom can feel a little messy at times. We experience both the blessing of Christ through one another and the pain of sin. But that is just another example of how the Kingdom is upside down, because the way to healing is through brokenness. In the Kingdom, we serve, we forgive, we bless, and we are generous. There is no getting around these things. It is the difference between the Kingdom of Jesus and our own rule and reign.

Being part of a Kingdom community is much more than going to the same church with the same people. A single church is just one small part of the Kingdom family in a town or neighborhood. Additionally, a Kingdom community does not require that everyone attend the same church. For example,

I'm okay going to church with people who worship like me and like the same kinds of services as I do. But the Kingdom community is bigger than my personal worship preferences. It needs to include people who are not like me. When I was at the wilderness ministry, we encouraged staff to attend different churches, depending on what worship style spoke to their hearts. We wanted people to know that their worship style or Bible study group was just a little piece of the larger disciplemaking community we all were a part of.

PERSONAL REFLECTION

Have you ever been part of a community that makes disciples? If not, have you heard or read about any? What are some of the characteristics you remember?

The people in the community of the Kingdom carry the glory and the fragrance of the King with them. It is recognizable to all people, even those outside the Kingdom.

That connection was immediately clear when I met some of the people who continue to disciple me to this day. When I first met Christine Caine, we were at the same meeting in New York, and to be honest, I did not know who she was. I don't have television and was not active on social media. All I know is that when I met her, I liked her. She did not know who I was either, but as we chatted, similar interests and pleasant conversation became something more. A charge came into the atmosphere. I call them *Kingdom sparkles*.[4] We knew we

---

[4] I think of these like spiritual lightning bugs or twinkling lights. They feel like sparkles in my heart.

were supposed to work together. How, we were not sure, but we started pursuing Kingdom relationship with one another, knowing the Lord would reveal the path.

The same thing happened with Alan Hirsch. Alan calls his experience of our conversations *Kingdom fireworks*.[5] In fact, this story has repeated many times. When I meet a Kingdom person, I often feel the Kingdom sparkles. It is a way of knowing and recognizing another person who serves under the kingship of Jesus and lives by the rules and values of the Kingdom of God. Those are the people I build life with and serve in ministry with. They are the people in my Kingdom community.

Finding Home

Recently I was on a trip with Andrew, my brother in the Lord. We had built the wilderness ministry together (along with Josh) but had not spent much time together in the last eight years. God had moved me on from the ministry, and the road took me to another state and whole other sphere of work. In our thirteen years working together, Andrew and I had spent thousands upon thousands of hours leading together, getting it right, getting it wrong, arguing, and wounding one another. We had truly lived like brother and sister.

Since I left the wilderness ministry, I have added regular therapy as part of my soul care routine. God has done so much through it. On our trip, I learned that Andrew had done the same, gaining healing for his soul in deep and surprising

---

[5] A person who has not had the revelation of brotherly and sisterly love might misunderstand the feeling of affection that comes with Kingdom sparkles. That is why the Kingdom is made manifest in community where we share in brotherly and sisterly love and are not so out of control with the lusts of the flesh that we miss the unity and affection of being joined in Christ.

ways. Though we had both wounded each other, in the years since, we had also both done the work to find greater wholeness and healing. We had both continued to be disciples of Jesus, letting him have greater lordship in our lives.

The change in us was amazing. We had experienced Kingdom together in the ministry, but on this trip there was a level of spiritual maturity and emotional health that I'd thought we would only know on the other side of eternity. It was beautiful.

Together, we were the brother and sister that I'd thought we would only get to be in heaven. Our lives of discipleship, of submitting to the lordship of Jesus, had made us better people. And we were able to enjoy healthy, deep, rich relationship with each other. Laughter and joy were abundant on that trip. I felt the rest that comes from being known and loved. *It was like coming home.* My brother, who had in some ways been estranged from me, was restored.

PERSONAL REFLECTION

Who do you long to be restored to? Who do you long to have a reconciled relationship with? If you could move toward greater spiritual maturity and emotional health, who would you want to do life with?

Once we experience the King and his Kingdom, it wrecks us, changes us, and inspires us repeatedly over a lifetime. Once we've experienced life with the King and Kingdom people, we can never be content with simply living a religious life.

Kingdom life and community is the reward of disciple-making. We can find health, maturity, and wholeness on this side of the veil. We can experience the Kingdom of God on earth, as it is in heaven. We don't have to wait. We can live the life God dreams of *right now*.

We existed in relationship with God at the beginning, and Jesus came so that relationship, that community with God, might be reconciled and restored. He came to bring us back home (1 Peter 3:18). The home the Trinity creates is called the Kingdom. It is the place where we are loved, accepted, and secure. It gives us a sense of belonging that tells us who we are.

And while this will be completed on the other side of eternity, how much of that home and Kingdom we experience on this side of eternity is up to us.

Discussion Questions

1. What part of the description of the Kingdom of God was new to you? What part of the Kingdom of God is the easiest for you to live out? What part is the hardest?

2. How can you, as a disciplemaking community, help broaden your awareness of the Kingdom and create avenues of participation with the Kingdom?

3. Have you ever been part of a Kingdom community or a spiritual place that felt like home? What do you remember about it? What was special about it? What would you like to re-create in your life with the people you disciple?

Inventory

At the beginning of the chapter, we looked at this Scripture passage:

> When I think of all this, I fall to my knees and pray to the Father, the Creator of everything in heaven and on earth. I pray that from his glorious, unlimited resources he will empower you with inner strength through his Spirit. Then Christ will make his home in your hearts as you trust in him. Your roots will grow down into God's love and keep you strong. And may you have the power to understand, as all God's people should, how wide, how long, how high, and how deep his love is. May you experience the love of Christ, though it is too great to understand fully. Then you will be made complete with all the fullness of life and power that comes from God.
>
> Now all glory to God, who is able, through his mighty power at work within us, to accomplish infinitely more than we might ask or think. Glory to him in the church and in Christ Jesus through all generations forever and ever! Amen.
>
> EPHESIANS 3:14-21, NLT

How does the Scripture sound to you now? What new meaning does it carry for you?

What revelations or insights are you taking away from this chapter? Capture them here:

Revelation/Insight #1

Revelation/Insight #2

LIVES CHANGED

EXPERIENCES REVELATION

LEARNS NEW THINGS

FEELS THE STRUGGLE

TEAMS WITH OTHERS

ANSWERS THE CALL

ORDINARY PERSON

DISCERNS THE SEASON

9

DISCERNS THE SEASON

Turning the Page

Be very sure now, you who have been trained to a self-sufficient maturity, that you enter into a generous common life with those who have trained you, sharing all the good things that you have and experience.

Don't be misled: No one makes a fool of God. What a person plants, he will harvest. The person who plants selfishness, ignoring the needs of others—ignoring God!—harvests a crop of weeds. All he'll have to show for his life is weeds! But the one who plants in response to God, letting God's Spirit do the growth work in him, harvests a crop of real life, eternal life.

So let's not allow ourselves to get fatigued doing good. At the right time we will harvest a good crop if we don't give up, or quit. Right now, therefore, every time we get the chance, let us work for the benefit of all, starting with the people closest to us in the community of faith.

GALATIANS 6:6-10, MSG

THE FIFTEEN-PASSENGER VAN BUMPED along the back country road, kicking up rocks and dirt. A cloud of dust hung inside the van from the open windows, but no one seemed to mind. The dust was preferable to the stench of thirteen adult bodies returning from forty days in the wilderness.

I always volunteered to go get the team. The drive took all day. It started at 5:00 a.m. with a three-hour drive on the interstate across southern Wyoming, followed by two hours on branching, unmarked dirt roads to the trailhead where wilderness-worn travelers met me with huge smiles. The five-hour drive back to the base was filled with stories and tales of challenges and revelations.

God had done so much in their lives, and hearing about it renewed my faith and restored my soul. As I listened, I wondered—where would they go from here? They were noticeably different from the people who had set out only forty days ago, but in many ways, their journey had just begun. They were forever changed by Jesus, and I could not wait to see what he had in store for them next.

Journey's End

At some point, the discipleship relationship must change and move on. You will not always be around, and you need to prepare the disciple for that. When your journey ends as their disciplemaker, the disciple continues on in a new chapter with new mentor-helpers. And though it is hard, you need to let them go. Because of the gift of your help, they get to stand on your shoulders and achieve greater things beyond where you could have led them. It is the bittersweet reward of being a good disciplemaker.

A disciplemaking relationship usually ends in one of three ways:

1. The disciple steps away from you and loses interest in the relationship.
2. The Lord releases you from being their disciplemaker.
3. The disciple graduates from the season of being mentored by you, in which case you can be friends even though you are no longer actively discipling them. Here, the relationship becomes like an adult child-and-parent relationship. It's still a relationship, but the dynamic is quite different.

On the first path, when the struggle comes, the disciple gets scared and backs up or retreats. Instead of letting God expose their heart and redeem it, they cover it up, hide from God, and pull the escape cord. You can encourage and support them, but you may not be able to stop them from leaving. If they do this, you just love them, bless them, and release them into God's hands. He is the author of their story, and he can find a way to reach them.

On the second path, the disciple just sits in the struggle, spinning. They don't quit, but they don't go forward either. They could be in the "stuck" place for a week or a year, and you may begin to wonder if God has something else for you as a disciplemaker.

A discipling relationship involves some level of both accountability and challenge, and people usually engage with the challenge or break off the relationship. But change can sometimes be slow. You don't want to cut the disciple off or leave them behind in your impatience right before they were about to turn the corner.

Remember, discipleship is not about efficient progress or wasting your time. It's not your time anyway. If God told you to disciple someone, then he is the one who must release you. And sometimes he doesn't. Sometimes he has you sit and wait, growing as a disciple yourself as you do.

When you are feeling frustrated or struggling with tension in the relationship, talk to God about it. The disciple may walk away and reject you, but that is between them and God. Your posture as a disciplemaker is to pray and champion them.

Only God knows when it's right to be long-suffering and when it's okay to be released. Come before the Lord with open hands, asking him if you are to persevere or if you are to let the disciple go. Be in dialogue with God about this, and he will guide you with peace.

The third way is that the disciple goes through the hard part, feels the struggle, and gains the revelation that God wants to give them. They yield to the challenge, surrender to what God is doing, and experience transformation. Those are my favorite stories of all. Those are summits worth celebrating.

The way you deal with disciplemaking transitions requires discernment. Relationships that end poorly can feel like rejection or even betrayal. But if things end well, be intentional to celebrate with a "rite of passage." Learning to navigate the different outcomes is a part of our own discipleship journey.

Betrayal or Rejection

One of the most painful experiences for the disciplemaker is when the person they are discipling—the one they are pouring their heart, time, and wisdom into—betrays or rejects them. I've been there myself, and it is heartbreaking. If you have experienced this already, or if you are hesitant about discipling someone because you are afraid of this, then you are in good company. Out of twelve disciples, Jesus was betrayed by one, and all but one of the rest left Jesus in the hard place. Jesus knows how much that hurts, and that is why he commits to never leaving us, no matter how hard or how dark things get.

What is a healthy and appropriate expectation when it comes to relational pain in disciplemaking? Struggling with and on behalf of others is part of the Kingdom and part of being identified with Christ. As Jesus says in Luke 9:23, to be a disciple, we must take up our cross and follow him. Discipleship is about laying down our agenda and picking up God's, laying down the story we would write for ourselves and picking up his story for us. You can avoid the hard thing God is asking you to do, but in doing so you are effectively opting out of being a disciple.

If we love people, our hearts will get hurt. But if we choose to protect ourselves from potential hurt, then we will never really love. I have chosen to love, lay down my life, and occasionally experience betrayal. But I don't regret a single piece of my heart that I have given away. Not that it is ever whole again. But that's okay; it doesn't have to be![1] While I don't have scars on my hands, feet, or side like Jesus, I have

---

[1] I learned this deep and profound lesson through four miscarriages. At the end of *The Lord of the Rings*, Frodo reflects that time does not heal all wounds. I have found this to be true, but there is a difference between choosing to be wounded and letting things be incompletely healed. I miss what I have lost because I have truly loved. And love is strong enough to coexist and eventually overshadow the pain. Regret is a choice. I choose to feel my life rather than be numb to it. After all, that is what it means to live an abundant life.

evidence of loving well and taking up my cross as a disciple and a disciplemaker.

PERSONAL REFLECTION

Sometimes when things get hard, the enemy tells us it is because we are inadequate. Think about Jesus for a moment. What were some of the struggles he had with his disciples? How might Jesus' struggles as a disciplemaker encourage you in the hard places?

Rites of Passage

The Jewish people mark seasonal changes with festivals— celebrations of what has been. Giving thanks to God and remembering his faithfulness encourages them that his faithfulness will follow into the next season as well.

Celebrations that mark seasonal changes are sometimes called "rites of passage." Graduation, a marriage ceremony, or even last rites are all moments when a community gathers to mark the transitions of life. As young people, we celebrate our graduations and weddings, filled with optimism, joy, and hope. As we grow older, watching our own children graduate and wed, the same celebrations of joy are intermixed with the grief of letting go.

Likewise, it is important to mark the seasons of change in our relationships with the people we disciple. If it is a positive transition, we celebrate what has been and how far they have come. If it ends with them leaving or God releasing us, it is healthy to grieve the loss of the relationship.

Let the Lord and your disciplemaker speak truth to you about the transition and seek healing for any wounds it may have caused.

PERSONAL REFLECTION

Take a moment and think about discipleship relationships in your past. Why did they end? How did they end? How do you feel about how they ended? Why?

Maturing in the Journey

Not too long ago I was on the phone with a person I was discipling. They were talking about a recurring argument with their spouse about money, jobs, and their living space. They were about to welcome a new child into the family, and they were feeling the pinch. One spouse worked from home while watching their other children and wondered about getting a different job that took more time but paid better. The other spouse worked a job that had good benefits but did not pay a high salary. They found themselves in a circular argument about needing a new home, the time it would take to look for and finance one, and whether they could even qualify.

I asked the person I was discipling all the things they were afraid of in the scenario. They listed about five or six fears that ran circles around their mind. Then I asked them what fears their spouse had expressed. Two or three additional fears came to light. There were a lot of places we could have started, but since the disciple needed to respond to a new job offer the next day, I cut right to it.

"Who is responsible for making sure your family is fed and has a roof over their head?" I asked.

The disciple paused, accustomed to my bluntness but sensing it was a trick question. "I know the right answer is Jesus, but I can't help feeling like my spouse and I are responsible and should be adults."

I said they were right, it was Jesus. That is what Jesus says in the Sermon on the Mount in Matthew. As parents and mature adults, their responsibility was to follow where Jesus was leading. That meant they needed to look at their life to see what Jesus was providing them and not what they were grasping at out of fear.

We talked through the different options and opportunities. As the disciple talked through each one, they were able to identify what was a faith-based option and what was a fear-based option. As a result, they turned down the job offer since they had pursued it out of fear, and they stepped out in faith in looking for a new home.

When I followed up with the disciple about a week later, I learned that God had already provided them with a new home they could afford on their current wages. The couple still had to remind each other of the truth about God when fears would come up, but their steps of faith were making a difference.

Through the pain and struggle, their understanding of God was tested, and their faith grew stronger. The challenge they faced was an opportunity to put into practice what they were learning. They learned to face their fears and move forward in obedience, and I followed up to find out how things went. Together, we walked the hard path, reached the mountain summit, and saw the goodness of God in the land of the living.

Passing along wisdom and watching others mature in their faith is one of the greatest joys of a disciplemaker. Paul expressed it this way: "He is the one we proclaim, admonishing and teaching everyone with all wisdom, so that we may present everyone fully mature in Christ" (Colossians 1:28, NIV). But how do we know when someone is ready to move on without us? What does it mean to be "mature"?

In the plant world, maturity is defined by *the ability to reproduce*. Fundamentally, immature plants cannot produce mature fruit, and immature fruit cannot reproduce anything. This means that a fruit is considered ripe and mature when it contains seeds that can reproduce new fruit-bearing plants. A mature strawberry has seeds that can be planted and will grow into strawberry bushes.[2] But if you plant the seeds of an immature strawberry, they will not be able to grow or reproduce. Why would the branches of the vine (John 15:1-14) be any different?[3] That's why a mature disciple makes disciples who go on to make more disciples.

The hard part is that you cannot produce spiritual maturity in another person. Rather, as we have discussed, it is a process of learning and unlearning, living and dying, building and baptism. It is climbing the mountain and coming back down again. We mature by being broken and remade. It is process based, not outcome based. God has always demonstrated that he is not focused on the outcome; that has been secure

---

[2] Botanical nerd fact: Strawberries are the only fruit with the seeds on the outside. Botany was my first degree and remains my first love academically.

[3] Grapevines must have their budding grapes (fruit) pruned off for up to three years so that the vine can grow strong enough to hold the weight of the ripe grapes. If the vinedresser doesn't do that, the growing grapes become too heavy for the vine and break off before they ripen. This is definitely something to think about, especially in light of the fact that Jesus spent three years discipling the Twelve.

since the beginning of time (Isaiah 46:9-10). But he is focused on the journey and walking us through the maturing process.

This is a really different way to think about discipleship rather than climbing a ladder of knowledge toward some sort of nondescript spiritual adulthood. Maturity is not what you know about God; it is about having a deep relationship with him. It is about discovering all the treasures/revelations he wants to show you and have you pass along to others. In this paradigm of disciplemaking, spiritual maturity is looking like Jesus and reproducing those who can help others look like Jesus.

Spiritual maturity in disciplemaking is . . .

Not	But
looking only to our own desires	death to self
a private, individual endeavor	being part of and accountable to a community
becoming smarter or wiser or better	giving what you have
checking boxes or having answers	journeying according to God's will and authorship of life
trying to do drive-through spirituality	embracing that disciplemaking is both simple and slow
mimicking the role models who let you down	being the role model/guide/mentor you wish you'd had
overcommitting and under delivering	being intentional to keep your disciplemaking process both simple and deep

Having these convictions as part of our overall paradigm of discipleship helps us see the bigger picture and better cooperate with God's rhythms. Just like trees and vines, we go through seasons, and each season has purpose in how it affects us and contributes to our overall maturation.

PERSONAL REFLECTION

How have you thought about spiritual maturity before? How do these descriptions cause you to think about spiritual maturity now? Is there anything you would like to add that you think is missing?

Seasons of the Hero's Journey

Like all things of God, discipleship has its own natural rhythm of beginning and ending. It has phases and seasons that can be recognized. Remember, disciplemaking has a map. We can figure out where we are, even when we don't know the exact route. Once again, the Hero's Journey can help us orient ourselves to where we are and discern where we're going.

PHASES OF BEING A DISCIPLEMAKER

Hero's Journey Phases	Disciplemaker's Activity
Ordinary Person	Anybody, any place, any time
Answers the Call	Partners with God for the conversation

Hero's Journey Phases	Disciplemaker's Activity
Teams with Others	Discerns who Holy Spirit is connecting you with.
Learns New Things	Listens to the disciple and Holy Spirit to discern how God is moving. Brings in content and tools as God leads.
Feels the Struggle	Champions the work of God. Encourages and supports the disciple to be brave as it gets hard.
Experiences Revelation	Waits on the Lord and prays for the disciple. Continues to be in the hard place with them and brings them courage.
Lives Changed	Observes the change in the disciple's life—names it and celebrates it
Discerns the Season	Recognizes when the season of discipleship is over.

Ordinary Person

We are all ordinary people on a journey, whether we know where we are on the map or not. God is pursuing each of us, so we can join him in that—any person, any place, any time. Maintain a posture of availability, listening to see who God might send you to.

Answers the Call

When we tune our ears to hear from God, we can begin to see how God is at work in our lives and the lives of the people around us. This allows us to join him in what he is doing. Joy and mutual affinity can happen when God draws people toward each other. He brings us together so that we might learn from and be shaped by one another. This may be the privilege of a onetime experience with a stranger, or God may be asking you to commit to journeying with someone for a period of time.

If God is drawing people toward you, pray and ask Holy Spirit if there is an intentional discipleship relationship to be formed, or whether you are just meant to be friends and peers. Ask Holy Spirit if you are to be intentional about meeting with the person regularly to discuss spiritual issues and to model what it looks like to follow Jesus. You can also ask Holy Spirit if there is a specific lesson or season from your life that might hold some treasures/revelations to share with them.

Teams with Others

As we team up with people, we recognize discipleship will look different with every person. For some, the season will be short; for others it can cover years, even decades. Your role with the same person might change over time. The first season, you might be more of a guide, whereas in later years, you're a friend helping them along the way.

Once the intentionality of the disciple/disciplemaker relationship is made known and you rope up to each other, the next step for the disciplemaker is to listen. The meetings or conversations are not about *downloading* your knowledge and wisdom. Instead, your job is to hear their stories, their heart, their pain, and listen for their hope.

This is really a three-way listening exercise. You are listening to the words they are saying. You are listening to the things they are not saying but mean to say, or whether they are putting a spin on something to make themselves look better. And you are listening to what Holy Spirit is saying about them. Remember, it is not your job to point out every little thing they are doing wrong or to correct every mis-understanding. *This is not how Holy Spirit models discipleship and disciples us.* Rather, listen, pray, make notes, ask questions, and listen more.

Learns New Things

As you hear Holy Spirit and discern what new idea, freedom, or breakthrough God wants to give the disciple, you can then begin to use content to help the disciple grow in the key areas God is highlighting. These could be Scripture, books, podcasts, sermons, or other resources. They are something to give you the biblical text, foundation, idea, or teaching to have conversation around. Regardless of your own maturity, it is important that you approach the conversation as a student yourself—as a fellow learner alongside the disciple. In exploring the content chosen, be a companion on the journey. This way you can learn old truths in a deeper way, gain new insights, or be refreshed by the amazing love and truth of God.

If you are working through a particular book, workbook, or series, stick with it until you've completed it, rather than make a change midstream. Sometimes we settle for the whipped cream and sprinkles on top of the sundae but miss the amazing, rich awesomeness that comes from a deep dive into the goodness of God.

Overall, this is the stable, building phase of discipleship. The disciple is working and growing, mirroring you through relationship. They are learning to reflect and asking good questions. You are sharing your revelations and helping them to process theirs. Day by day and step-by-step, the miles move behind you.

Feels the Struggle

But the steady pace of movement does not last forever. As you listen and hear the heart of the disciple for God and the heart of God for the disciple, eventually you begin to see the deeper issues in the disciple's life that hinder growth. You see where they have constructed patterns of behavior or thoughts that are not life-giving or don't line up with Scripture. Patterns, real fears, real hopes, real places of growth will emerge.

As a disciplemaker, you begin to challenge the disciple more, pushing them to face their issue or to take steps to deal with their

Disciplemaker Pro Tip:

As you walk through the content with the disciple, help them to think through what they are learning and the revelation God is bringing, so that it leads to *transformation*, rather than just the accumulation of information. As a reminder from chapter 5, here's the pathway for helping the disciple to grow:

1. Discern the internal process (character to be formed): *What is God doing to bring greater wholeness and how can the disciple participate in/with that?*

2. Discern the external process (obedience to be walked out): *What is the response that will help them live toward that?*

3. Ask why and a follow-up question.

4. Repeat.

heart and behavior. The relationship can become tense. As a disciplemaker, you continue to invest in this person—caring for them and wanting what is best for them. You may feel like a broken record or that you are hitting your head against a wall. The disciple may feel like they have heard all you have to say and are receiving less from the relationship.

Remember, sometimes a person's most obvious growth point is not the one God is most concerned about. Sometimes there is a deeper or more harmful issue in their heart that God wants to address. As we learned in chapter 7, this is the big challenge of the mountain, not the distracting false summits. I believe that God is less concerned with sinful behavior than whether we trust him or think he is good (Romans 4:5). God wants to draw us closer to his heart rather than merely conform the way we act (Galatians 2:16). When love is the central paradigm of the discipleship relationship, you will discern what the disciple should move away *from* and help them discern what God is drawing them *toward*.

This is where you need to be present and patient, even more dependent upon God yourself. This is also where you can inspire courage in the disciple, letting them know that God is for them, and you are there to help them. This will be important because you cannot take the next step of the journey for them. They must choose it for themselves.

Experiences Revelation

Deep transformation happens in the unseen. When a sword is first being formed, it must be tested to see what has melted into the sword and become part of it, and what has not bonded and will easily break away. Likewise, the disciple must be tested to see what they have truly learned. What internal pathways have truly been made new? What deep convictions have formed and revelations been birthed?

This is how character is forged as part of God's faithfulness to us. This is how we are made new again and how we know that we know something—because it has been tried and proven true.

Challenges and struggles reveal what we believe. As a disciplemaker, this is where you wait, pray, and encourage. This is where an ordinary person becomes a hero, and a disciple is changed by Jesus.

Lives Changed

Though it can feel like it, the struggle does not last forever. The earth turns, the days pass by, and we walk out the other side of the wilderness. The disciple is a different person because they have encountered the resurrected Jesus. (And we, the disciplemaker and guide, are a little bit older and probably a little bit grayer.) The disciple is living with a new love for Christ and his Kingdom. Their identity is reformed and they are experiencing freedom where there once was bondage. The deep change that has happened in the heart of the disciple is revealed in their relationships with those around them. The work of God proves itself as they live life in a new way. Both their trust and your trust in God deepens as you see that he is faithful and good. The question that lies before you is, "What's next?"

Discerns the Season

As a disciplemaker you have witnessed the greatest miracle heaven has to offer: a changed heart. It is worth celebrating!

Unlike a habit or behavior, heart change is something that is not easily forgotten. Revelations are hard to unlearn.

The disciple now has a revelation of God and a testimony to share. And it is God's will that they do so. They have been through a portion of the wilderness. Now God invites them to guide others who might find themselves in that same portion as well.

The next season in your relationship with the disciple is a new question to lay before God: How should it change, and how should it stay the same? Sometimes God leads you to journey with the disciple through another season, having you mentor them as they mentor someone else.

But often, God has something different in mind. Often, he has a new season for the disciple, full of new lessons. So they need a new guide. And God may be drawing another person toward you who needs the lessons you are good at guiding someone through. Neither of those changes means you are not close any more, but it does mean things will be different, and that's okay. Remember, disciplemaking is a community activity, so you can embrace the season change and let each other move forward with the grace of God. Disciplemaking is about recognizing God-ordained seasons and asking Spirit-led questions. For many years I have watched the cycle of discipleship play out repeatedly. God is faithful to the pattern of it, although the length of each season varies.

God brings people together to journey with one another for a time. They have their adventures together, and then the season changes and the nature of the relationship evolves. Whether discipleship is one-on-one or with a small group of people, teasing out the natural phases of the disciple/

disciplemaker relationship helps us better walk alongside others, according to God's design.

PERSONAL REFLECTION

Take a moment and think about either your life as a disciple or someone you are currently discipling. What part of the journey do you think you are in right now?

Bearing Seeds

Not too long ago, my husband and I sat with the neighbors who make up our house church. We are a small, interdenominational group. Our monthly gatherings consist of dinner, personal check-ins about what God is doing in our lives, and prayer for one another. When it was my turn to "check in," I reached in my pocket and pulled out a set of small jewelry sachets, each containing ten dry pinto beans, and handed them out to everyone.

"I have been thinking for a while about how to express my gratitude for and commitment to sharing life with each of you," I said as they passed around the transparent little sacks. "I wanted to come up with something that would symbolize my commitment to invest life and love into you. Each of these sacks has ten pinto beans. When I was a high school biology teacher, I learned you could take dry pinto beans from the grocery store and get them to sprout and grow. That is important to me because I wanted the symbol of my connection to you to be a living one, one that could reproduce."

As they each looked at the little bags, I continued, "Thank

you for the honor and privilege of letting me know and love you. I don't take it for granted, and I am profoundly moved each time I think of the gift you are to me."

I must admit, I got a little emotional. Some of them did as well.

"But here is the catch," I said. "I want each of you to think about who *you* want to invest your life and love into—who you want to hand these beans to. Who do you want to commit to pouring into? Who do you want to say thank you to for letting you impact them? Who do you want to commit to sharing the love of Jesus with?"[4]

In the movie *Avengers: Endgame*, Tony Stark leaves a message to his wife where he reflects that "part of the journey is the end." This is true of all adventures, including the hero maker's journey. Stories end, fellowships part, and seasons change. The end is what makes life and the journey precious.

But your story still goes on. What you do after turning this last page is up to you. How big of an adventure are you willing to go on with God? What kind of summits would you like to climb, or sunsets would you like to experience with God?

Disciplemaking is simple but not easy. You'll go through hard and challenging times, but you'll also experience

---

[4] Here is how you can do the same simple activity:
1. Buy some dry beans from the store. (I would recommend something bigger than lentils).
2. Gather some little bags (snack-size plastic baggies or little jewelry bags).
3. Hand out the little sacks of beans.
4. Express your gratitude to those who have allowed you to be part of their story and Hero's Journey. Be specific about what treasures you see in them.
5. Ask them who in their life they would like to intentionally invest in and express gratitude for. Have them think about it for a moment.
6. Challenge them to repeat the symbolic gesture (including the challenge to repeat themselves).

amazing moments that make the cost worth it. It is up to you. Your willingness to open your heart will directly correspond to your effectiveness as a disciplemaker. You can guard yourself and keep yourself protected, or you can take the risk that love demands. It is a scary thing, but Jesus has gone first. It is up to you how far you will follow him.

Discussion Questions

1. How does thinking about discipleship in terms of season change the goal of disciplemaking?

2. What is your role as a disciplemaker in the change you wish to see in the disciple? How do you help it? How might you hinder it?

3. How long do you think change takes? How can you be sure it is happening?

4. What can you, as a community, do to help each other with the scale of discipleship? How can you work together to support those who are wanting to be discipled?

5. How can you help others answer the call to be a disciplemaker?

Inventory

At the beginning of the chapter, we looked at this Scripture passage:

> Be very sure now, you who have been trained to a self-sufficient maturity, that you enter into a generous common life with those who have trained you, sharing all the good things that you have and experience.
>
> Don't be misled: No one makes a fool of God. What a person plants, he will harvest. The person who plants selfishness, ignoring the needs of others—ignoring God!—harvests a crop of weeds. All he'll have to show for his life is weeds! But the one who plants in response to God, letting God's Spirit do the growth work in him, harvests a crop of real life, eternal life.
>
> So let's not allow ourselves to get fatigued doing good. At the right time we will harvest a good crop if we don't give up, or quit. Right now, therefore, every time we get the chance, let us work for the benefit of all, starting with the people closest to us in the community of faith.
>
> GALATIANS 6:6-10, MSG

How does the Scripture sound to you now? What new meaning does it carry for you?

What revelations or insights are you taking away from this chapter? Capture them here:

Revelation/Insight #1

Revelation/Insight #2

NavPress is the book-publishing arm of The Navigators.

Since 1933, The Navigators has helped people around the world bring hope and purpose to others in college campuses, local churches, workplaces, neighborhoods, and hard-to-reach places all over the world, face-to-face and person-by-person in an approach we call Life-to-Life® discipleship. We have committed together to know Christ, make Him known, and help others do the same.®

Would you like to join this adventure of discipleship and disciplemaking?

- Take a Digital Discipleship Journey at **navigators.org/disciplemaking**.
- Get more discipleship and disciplemaking content at **thedisciplemaker.org**.
- Find your next book, Bible, or discipleship resource at **navpress.com**.

 @NavPressPublishing

 @NavPress

 @navpressbooks

CP1790